Joan Phillips

POLICING THE FAMILY

Social control in Thatcher's Britain

junius

Phillips, Joan
  Policing the family: social control in Thatcher's Britain.
  1. Great Britain. Families. Policies of government.
  I. Title

  362.8'256'0941
  ISBN 0-948392-10-X

Published March 1988
Typeset by Junius Publications Ltd
Printed by Blackrose (TU)
Copyright © Junius Publications BCM JPLtd, London WC1N 3XX
01-729 0414

CONTENTS

CONTENTS

Preface

For nine years Margaret Thatcher's Conservative government has set the agenda of British politics. Thatcher's success has rested above all on her ability to force her opponents to retreat on to Tory territory. The signal achievement of the Thatcher years has been the Tories' victories on the ideological front. The battle of ideas has been fought largely on the field of morality. Today the Tories might appear vulnerable on the economic front, but their moral armoury appears unassailable.

Two weeks into 1988 *The Times* reflected on the success of Britain's rulers in shifting public opinion on to the high moral ground:

'The annual survey of national habits and attitudes published today by the government statistical service [Central Statistical Office, *Social Trends 1987*] paints, on the face of it, a dire picture of national depravity. Britain is a nation of pleasure-seekers, fleeing from the churches to the television and the gambling machine.

'Its citizens hold the marriage bond in increasing contempt and produce an unprecedented number of illegitimate children. They show scant respect for the law and expend much energy in the commission of crime. It may seem something of a paradox that a country whose politics are presided over by Mrs Thatcher, with her articulate devotion to Victorian values, should display so many of the characteristics traditionally, though inaccurately, attributed to Sodom and Gomorrah.

'The survey, however, presents an even more striking paradox. Much evidence from opinion polls suggest that public attitudes to personal morality are becoming increasingly conservative. The young tend to blame their parents for having brought them up too permissively; scourges such as Aids are regarded as the natural consequence of sexual licence; there is said to be a demand for more authoritative leadership from the churches. Yet the daily round of fornication and self-indulgence continues unabated.' (14 January 1988)

While conceding the advance of moral decay in British society, *The Times* applauds Thatcher's achievement in inculcating the values of conformity. No doubt *The Times* leader writer exaggerates the extent to which Tory prejudice has been taken on board by ordinary people. But there is much evidence to support his contention that a moral revival of some sort has taken place.

Until now the establishment has made all the running and the debate has remained one-sided. This book aims to change this state of affairs by challenging the official moral orthodoxy, and providing a radical alternative to the Tories' presentation of sexuality and morality.

Chapter 1 sets the revival of traditional morality in the context of British capitalist decline. It looks at how the Tories' success in promoting their moral panics has led to a growing acceptance of state interference in the lives of ordinary people. Chapter 2 focuses on the family as the central theme of establishment propaganda, and explains its function in modern society. It demystifies the current obsession with child abuse, and points to the dangers for the authorities in stepping up their policing role. Finally it offers a working class approach to the problems of family life.

Chapter 3 explores the history of state regulation of sexuality and morality, and highlights the tendency towards increasing repression. It examines the legal framework through which the ruling class exercises social control, and looks at the many agencies established to watch over the working class. It identifies the dangers of allowing the state such scope for intervention, and argues that a resistance movement is long overdue. Chapter 4 shows how abortion has become a key issue in the debate about morality. It exposes the hypocrisy of the anti-abortion lobby, and emphasises the necessity to make the issue of women's rights the focus of the opposition.

A central theme of the book is the failure of the left to offer a coherent challenge to the new moralists. Yet if we are to build a movement that can beat our enemies, we have got to make our voices heard with arguments that are irrefutable. The book ends with a platform of working class demands that provides the basis for turning the tables on the moral rearmers. For those who are committed to fighting for an end to oppression and for real freedom, there is now no choice but to go on the offensive.

Joan Phillips
London
February 1988

1.
Their morals and ours

Lt is a paradox of the Thatcher regime that a government which has railed against state intervention should have done more than any of its predecessors to increase the powers of the state over our lives. Nowhere is this more apparent than in the sphere of sexual and moral behaviour and family life. Since 1979 three Tory governments have mobilised the courts, the social services, the police, the welfare system, the churches and the media to promote the values of discipline and conformity inside and outside the home.

In Thatcher's Britain social workers are given powers to assume custody of children before they are born. A judge declares that a 14-year old rape victim is 'a menace to young men'. Parliament debates a host of measures to restrict abortion rights. The church hierarchy gives God's blessing to the persecution of homosexuals. Local authority and health service administrators gain access to criminal records to vet potential employees working with children. Censorship of television, films and videos extends social control into the living room. Customs and excise officials seize books destined for gay bookshops because they are judged obscene. The self-appointed moral guardians in the media issue prohibitions against behaviour beyond the bounds of public decency.

Over the past nine years Britain's rulers have succeeded in creating a new moral climate. Today state interference in wide areas of people's lives has come to be regarded as acceptable. The moral policemen of the established order point to an endless catalogue of social evils to justify the increasingly repressive activities of officialdom.

The press and television are full of scare stories about parents who batter their babies, gays and prostitutes who are said to spread the 'Aids plague', perverts who run child sex rackets, teenagers who take the pill and indulge in promiscuous sex, women who have abortions so they can go on holiday and evil doctors who experiment with human embryos. If we took seriously the preoccupations of the media, we would feel ourselves to be at constant risk from gun-toting psychopaths, football hooligans, drug addicts, invading immigrants, Stonehenge hippies, surrogate mothers and foreign terrorists. Let's look at some of the issues that have dominated the recent debate.

● **Child abuse**

'Child abuse is the biggest blot on civilised life' declared Margaret Thatcher in her traditional New Year message. The old year ended with the police claiming to have smashed the 'biggest ever' child pornography ring in London and the home counties, and another child sex and pornography racket in Congleton, Cheshire. The nation was horrified by the findings of the inquiries into the deaths of four-year old Kimberly Carlile, who was burned, battered and starved to death by her stepfather in July 1986, and 21-month old Tyra Henry, who was beaten and bitten to death by her father in August 1984. The National Society for the Prevention of Cruelty to Children issued alarming statistics about the increase in crimes against children, reinforcing fears about an epidemic of child abuse.

From June through to December of 1987, not a day went by without the papers adding some new twist to the Cleveland child sex abuse controversy. The almost monthly re-enactment of the Moors murders in the tabloid press must rank as the ultimate child abuse case. More than 20 years after Ian Brady and Myra Hindley were convicted for the murder of three children whose bodies were found in shallow graves on Saddleworth Moor, the media insists on subjecting the families of the deceased and the public to the gruesome details. The awful crimes of Brady and Hindley are summoned up to remind people of the human capacity for evil and to satisfy the media craze for child abuse.

- **Homosexuality**

'The law of the land allows consenting adult homosexuals to engage in sexual practices which I think should be criminal offences,' declared Manchester police chief James Anderton in an end-of-year outburst. 'Sodomy between males is an abhorrent offence, condemned by the word of God, and ought to be against the criminal law' (*Woman's Own,* 19 December 1987). Anderton, who has earned notoriety for his outspoken bigotry and his claim to be God's prophet, had earlier caused uproar when he stated that criminals should be flogged until they begged for mercy. But his pronouncements about the 'abomination' of homosexuality scarcely raised an eyebrow. God's cop may widely be regarded as a crank, but his backward views about homosexuality have become common currency in the Britain of the late eighties.

The anti-gay consequences of the government's obscure icebergs and exploding mountains commercial about Aids at the beginning of 1987 were not widely apparent. But by the end of the year the purpose of the government's legislation to outlaw 'the promotion of homosexuality' was clear to all. In the intervening months the press ran a witch-hunt against fallen pop idol Elton John over allegations of homosexual orgies. Tory MP Harvey Proctor was forced to resign over scandals involving rent boys and spanking sessions. Deceased former MI5 chief Maurice Oldfield was condemned in various serialised memoirs for his 'compulsive homosexuality'. Pop star Freddie Mercury was 'exposed' as a drug-crazed gay whose friends were all dropping dead from Aids.

The Church of England reaffirmed its opposition to homosexuality at its November Synod, and later applauded the Bishop of Ripon's decision to refuse to ordain practising gay vicars. Thatcher awarded the fanatically anti-gay chief rabbi, Emmanuel Jakobovits, a seat in the house of lords. The Labour Party did its bit by blaming the left's focus on lesbian and gay rights for its disastrous electoral performances, and Neil Kinnock attacked left-wing education authorities for trying to 'impose' positive images of homosexuality on school students. To round off a year of 'queer-bashing', the BBC prepared a last exit for *EastEnders* gays Colin and Barry. In keeping with the official teaching on what should be done with homosexuals, Colin and Barry will either be 'straightened out' or given the boot.

- **The nation's youth**

'Young people are crying out for a set of rules and standards to live by,' declared Margaret Thatcher at the start of the year. 'It is up to us to restore them' (*Sun,* 4 January 1988). The prime minister was speaking on one of her favourite subjects: the threat to the flower of the nation's youth from the decline of Christian standards in schools, on television and at home. Over the past year panics about juvenile crime, sex and violence on the small screen and adolescent drug abuse have served as a focus for anxiety about the degeneracy of 'young people today'. Commenting on the record crime figures in March, former Metropolitan Police chief Kenneth Newman drew attention to the responsibility of teachers and parents for disciplining the nation's youth: 'They [the crime statistics] must reflect on the extent to which schools have been successful in inculcating values and the extent to which parents have succeeded in bringing up law-abiding children.'

Moral campaigner Mary Whitehouse blames the media for corrupting young people. Starting the New Year as she means to carry on, Whitehouse wrote to BBC chiefs complaining of the 'chronic excesses' of programmes such as *EastEnders* and the time it is broadcast (7.30pm). She criticised scripts which included drug-taking, attempted suicide, promiscuity, endless lying, quarrelling, prostitution, blackmail, drunkenness, homosexual relations, bad language, violence and children watching pornographic videos. Whitehouse has seized a good moment to get her message across, after a year of raging debate about the effect of television violence on impressionable young minds. Meanwhile, the long-running scare about drug abuse and the government advertising campaign against it have encouraged grim forecasts of a generation of drug-crazed outcasts stalking the inner-city streets. Tory politicians blame the 'heroin epidemic' on the lack of discipline in schools and the collapse of parental authority.

The sexual abuse of children, the depravity of homosexuals and the spread of juvenile delinquency are all familiar themes of the anti-permissive moralists and law and order enthusiasts. Moral panics are not a new phenomenon, nor is their subject matter. From time to time in the past, Britain's rulers have stirred up popular prejudice against a perceived threat to the nation's well-being, and sponsored panics which bear a remarkable similarity to the preoccupations of our own modern-day moralists.

• 'Juvenile depravity'

'A bane to society, which like an ulcer on the body, is continually enlarging, and distributing far and wide its noxious influence...a general and latent depravity, which a large extent of juvenile depravity seems to indicate, is a state under which the manufacture of a nation must eventually decline, agriculture languish, and commerce disappear.'

The Reverend Henry Worsley's prize-winning essay, *Juvenile Depravity* (1849), summed up the early Victorian establishment's obsession with juvenile crime, and hinted at its fears of impending social collapse. The images of pollution and moral contagion might not be quite to Mrs Thatcher's taste, but, judging from her New Year speech on the squalor of our inner cities, she is not averse to using dirt as a metaphor for urban disorder in the manner of her Victorian counterparts.

Worsley was not alone in his horror of the offspring of 'the dangerous classes'. In 1843 Lord Ashley, Earl of Shaftesbury ('friend' of boy chimney-sweeps), rose before the house of commons to urge the necessity of a system of elementary schooling for this 'fearful multitude of untutored savages'. 'The morals of children are tenfold worse than formerly,' he declared as he presented evidence from different parts of the country. In Leeds 'the spirit of lawless insubordination' was 'a matter for painful apprehension'. In Birmingham 'sexual connection' began as early as 14 or 15 years of age. In the mining districts there were girls who 'drink, swear, fight, smoke, whistle, sing, and care for nobody'. In Manchester he encountered 'a vast number of children of the tenderest years' who 'roam at large through the streets of the town, contracting the most idle and profligate habits' (cited in Geoffrey Pearson, *Hooligan: A History of Respectable Fears*, 1983).

Ashley blamed the 'vicious habits' of the parents for this state of affairs. 'Is not every juvenile delinquent the evidence of a family in which the family bond is weakened and loosened?' declared Edward Irving in *The Last Days* in 1829. Writing in 1846, Walter Buchanan thought that the parents of juvenile criminals 'care no more for their offspring than hyenas for their whelps after they are suckled'. The more liberal members of the ruling class advocated moral and religious education for the new generation of workers to instil a proper respect for the law, property and order among the masses. Taking heed of the social convulsions and revolutionary ferment that swept through Europe in 1848, Thomas Beggs in his *Inquiry into the Extent and Causes of Juvenile Depravity* (1849) cautioned that steps must be taken to improve the moral condition of the poor. Henry Worsley also considered moral leadership to be the best safeguard against political disaffection. The link drawn by the early Victorians between juvenile immorality and national decline finds many contemporary echoes.

- ● **Victorian vice**

'England has tolerated the man Wilde for too long....He was a social pest, a centre of intellectual corruption...who attacked all wholesome, manly, simple ideals of English life.' (*Evening News,* 27 May 1895)

This was the *Evening News'* verdict on the fate of Oscar Wilde, the celebrated playwright and author, who was found guilty of 'acts of gross indecency' under the 1885 Criminal Law Amendment Act in a case that scandalised the late Victorian public. It could have been the *Sun* passing sentence on Elton John last year, over his alleged participation in homosexual orgies at a friend's country mansion. The pillorying of Oscar Wilde took place in the midst of a crusade for social purity which targeted homosexuality and prostitution as a threat to race and nation. The witch-hunt against Elton John took off in a climate of creeping reaction in which deviancy (homosexuality) and disease (Aids) have been depicted as omens of national disaster.

The Salvation Army signalled the start of the social purity movement in July 1885 when it launched a nationwide campaign against juvenile prostitution. The newly established popular press moulded public opinion, combining moral outrage and lurid titillation about the trade in teenage sex (how little has changed in Fleet Street and Wapping!). Papers like the *Pall Mall Gazette* pressed the Liberal government of William Gladstone to enact legislation to outlaw obscenity, indecency and prostitution. The campaign to promote conventional morality won support from a broad coalition of clergymen, politicians, purists, feminists and radicals. (For a full treatment of the social purity movement see Frank Mort, *Dangerous Sexualities: Medico-moral Politics in England since 1830,* 1987.)

The emergence of the purity movement coincided with a growing establishment concern about the urban poor. The prevalence of poverty and disease and the growing labour movement agitation, as well as unrest in Ireland, Egypt, India and other colonies, all contributed to widespread alarm in official circles about the immorality of the impoverished masses and its consequences for the Empire. In 1883 Andrew Mearns' *The Bitter Cry of Outcast London* exposed a vast mass of moral corruption and Godlessness at the centre of the metropolis. The moral purity campaigners directed their sanitising zeal at the working class, but they also focused popular discontent against the immorality and decadence of the aristocracy. Their message was that the purification of national life was a matter of importance which ranked above class differences and the petty divisions of party politics. There are some striking parallels between the social purity campaign of the 1880s-90s, and the new morality of the 1980s, not least their emphasis on the need for tougher intervention by the state to stamp out vice.

There are other well-documented moral panics. A more recent example occurred in the immediate post-war period when the authorities invoked anti-communist hysteria against the 'Red menace'. Although Cold War agitation never assumed the same dimensions in Britain as it did in the USA, the establishment fuelled a popular backlash against the communist 'threat' to national security. The list of disloyal elements extended from Soviet sympathisers and trade union militants, to take in homosexuals, drug users, drunks and those who indulged in 'loose living'. The government introduced a system of positive vetting to weed out such 'character defects' among employees in the civil service and the defence industry. Subsequent events have shown that this was entirely ineffective in weeding out spies, though thousands of ordinary workers lost their jobs. The anti-communist purge spread into the trade unions and political parties too.

Moral panics have certain common features. They play on insecurities arising from real social problems, and stir up irrational fears against the particular target of official prejudice. Moral panics seek to rally a wide consensus of support behind the establishment viewpoint. They encourage a climate favourable to repressive measures. But *why* does the establishment put such a premium on morality?

The cement of morality

To make sense of today's moral panics we have to examine the role of morality in the context of a society divided into antagonistic social classes. Capitalism is a system based on exploitation and oppression enforced by the rule of a small minority over the rest of society. Conventional morality helps the ruling class to disguise the evils of the system and to make these appear inevitable and inescapable to the majority who suffer them.

The development of capitalism in Britain in the early years of the nineteenth century involved profound upheaval. Capitalism advanced through a struggle against local and regional barriers to establish a national economy and a national market. The elimination of restrictions and the foundation of the nation state enabled the capitalist class to establish a nationwide division of labour which created the framework for innovation and growth. For many who lived through this experience, however, the rewards of the march of progress always seemed to be gathered by somebody else.

The rise of the world's first industrial nation entailed the destruction of traditional communities and the break-up of social conventions. Industrial development led to the demise of village-based rural life and the growth of city slums, the replacement of the old domestic crafts by modern manufacture, the extinction of the artisan and the dissolution of old customs. The generation which lived through the industrial revolution witnessed the rise of a ruthless new employing class which repudiated the responsibility to protect the poor which had been accepted by the old landowning elite. Workers experienced more intense exploitation, the misery and squalor of urban life, and insecurity of employment.

The process of social transformation unleashed at the start of the last century has carried on up to today. Capital accumulation necessitates the uprooting of individuals and the rupture of families. The expropriation of the agricultural producer from the land, through the violence of enclosure and land clearance, was necessary for industrialisation to proceed. The displaced peasantry was driven from the countryside to seek work in the mills and factories. In the 1950s the large-scale influx of immigrant labour into Britain was dictated by the demands of the post-war economy. Today the unemployed of Liverpool or Newcastle are forced to migrate to the building sites of Docklands or the service industries of the western corridor to earn a living.

The break-up of the family is a characteristic consequence of capitalist development. The onset of industrialisation heralded the dissolution of the old family ties, by bringing women and children into the factories and mines. Immigration—and Britain's immigration laws—have broken up countless families in Britain's former colonies. Mass unemployment over the past decade has placed intolerable strains on many working class families, leading to rising rates of separation and divorce.

The role of morality in capitalist society arises from its fundamentally exploitative and competitive character. Some individuals—a small class of capitalists—own the means of production, land, raw materials, machinery and factories. Others—the working class—own only their ability to work. In theory workers are free to choose whether or not to sell their capacity to work. In practice there is no other way they can survive. Workers need jobs because working for wages is the only way to earn a living in modern society for the vast majority of people. The capitalist puts the worker to work with the means of production: the product of the worker's labour thus becomes the capitalist's property. The capitalist ensures that the value of the products his employees make is greater than the value he pays out for means of production and wages. He does this by paying his workers less than the value they create. The free exchange between the worker and the capitalist thus conceals the exploitation of the worker in production. This relation of exploitation, which is reproduced day in day out, week in week out, year after year, generation after generation, lies at the root of the conflict between workers and capitalists.

As well as dividing society into two major classes, the capitalist system also sets worker against worker, and capitalist against capitalist. The conditions of capitalist exploitation drive members of the working class to join together in trade unions to defend their common interests. But workers are also forced to compete with one another in the battle for survival. Nurses are set against hospital ancillary workers, men fight to preserve differentials over women, white workers often turn a blind eye to discrimination against blacks, the unemployed resent those who are lucky enough to have work. The capitalist class is united in its determination to maintain its domination of society. But individual capitalists are also forced to compete with each other for markets and resources. In the capitalist marketplace, firms that cannot compete go to the wall.

In a society torn by division and conflict, norms which were once obligatory upon all lose their force. The old shared values which once acted to hold society together appear increasingly irrelevant. Modern capitalist society individualises and atomises people, and makes them less susceptible to universal codes of behaviour. The capitalist class is thus confronted with the problem of how to maintain social control—this is where morality comes in.

The ruling class of the early nineteenth century was obsessed with the immorality of 'the dangerous classes'. Social commentators and politicians labelled as immoral aspects of working class behaviour which threatened to disrupt the established order. These included drunkenness and promiscuity, family breakdown, declining church attendance, political radicalism and general disrespect for authority. Such behaviour defied the standards of sobriety, family respectability, piety, deference and industriousness, which were required of a disciplined working class.

The early philanthropists blamed industrialisation for the moral decline of the masses. 'The factory system,' said Samuel Smiles in 1843, 'however much it may have added to the wealth of the country, has had a most deleterious effect on the domestic condition of the people. It has invaded the sanctuary of the home and broken up the family and social ties' (Samuel Smiles, *Character*, 1879). The establishment tended to blame the innate depravity of the lower orders for the wretchedness of their condition.

The capitalist class instinctively recognised that to maintain discipline it had to establish a new set of social norms. Moral reform became a central component of its drive to assert control over society. The Victorian upper classes launched a crusade to train the working class in a new morality anchored around the sanctity of the family and the nation. The intimate connection between family morality and national well-being—a consistent feature of Thatcherite ideology today—was established early in the nineteenth century.

The philosopher Edmund Burke expounded the Victorian view of the organic link between family values and patriotism: 'To love the little platoon we belong to in society is the first link in the series by which we proceed to a love of our country and of mankind.' For the new morality, any threat to the family also jeopardised the nation. 'When shall we learn,' wrote Ellice Hopkins, a prominent purity feminist, 'that whoever touches the higher life and well-being of the family still more vitally affects the wider family of the state and threatens its disintegration' (Ellice Hopkins, *The Power of Womanhood: or Mothers and Sons,* 1899). We can find the same theme in the writings of today's right-wing moralists: 'If my imagination finds the lyric intensity it needs in the life of the family,' writes Richard Cronin, 'in the life of the nation it finds an epic scope' (*Salisbury Review,* September 1987).

The need to re-create norms that uphold the family and the nation is particularly important in a period of upheaval. In times of crisis the establishment has always sought to construct a moral consensus to strengthen its grip over society. Today, in conditions of economic instability and social unrest, the ruling class is especially keen to re-assert conventional values. In an editorial calling for a 'campaign for moral renewal', the *Daily Telegraph* spelt out the meaning of the new morality:

'No nation can flourish for long without some sort of moral consensus among its people. It is the consciousness of such a common outlook on matters of fundamental importance which holds civil society together and unites its members in the mutual affection which is called patriotism.' (*Daily Telegraph*, 4 June 1986)

The chief function of the official morality is social control. In a society which depends on the subordination of a majority of workers to a minority of exploiters, morality is the cement which holds society together. A morality which purports to serve the best interests of the whole of society acts to suppress conflicts between rival social classes. We are taught to put aside our own selfish concerns in the cause of the common good.

There is nothing natural or eternal about morality. Different societies at different times follow radically different codes of behaviour. Nor is morality neutral. Morality is the product of social development, and it serves the interests of the ruling class in society. The legal and moral codes of modern Western society are fashioned to suit the requirements of the capitalist system. The legal system upholds the sanctity of capitalist property. The moral code decrees that women carry the burden of toil in the home and accept a second class role in the world of work. The chief merit of the new morality for the capitalist class is that it dresses up submission and slavery in the language of common sense and righteousness. Thatcher's Victorian values are nothing more than an apology for exploitation and oppression.

The responsible family

The effect of today's moral crusade is to reconcile the working class to the consequences of the decay of British capitalism. The authorities have played on the insecurities arising from the recession to popularise their backward-looking views. The pressing theme of the establishment crusade is that something must be done to arrest the nation's moral decline. The immediate result has been more regimentation of the lives of ordinary people.

At a time of mass unemployment, growing poverty and disintegrating social services, Thatcher's re-assertion of traditional morality plays a vital role in demobilising resistance to the system. 'We now realise that the great problems in life are not those of housing, food and the standard of living,' declared Thatcher in a recent interview in *Woman's Own*. 'When you've got all those, you're still left with the problems of human nature' (31 October 1987). The

Tories' success in spreading panics about everything from child abuse to teenage promiscuity has led people to blame the evils resulting from the capitalist system on nature rather than on the way society is run.

The Tories have focused attention on the threat to traditional values because they recognise the vital role that the family can play in holding society together. This is why the promotion of the family underpins all the major panics of the Thatcher years, from scares about surrogate motherhood to scandals about extramarital sex.

Thatcher has tried to promote the family as a bulwark of conservatism in an age of instability. Family life emphasises individual preoccupations at the expense of collective action. Politicians, priests and television commentators constantly encourage people to put their families first, before their union, party or class. The message of the new morality is that the individual and the family, not society, must take responsibility for sorting out their problems. 'You know, there is no such thing as society,' proclaimed Thatcher. 'There are individual men and women, and there are families' (*Woman's Own,* 31 October 1987).

A nation of families, as Thatcher well knows, is a collection of private individuals. As long as every individual man and woman is preoccupied with sorting out their own immediate problems themselves, Thatcher's system is safe, and that's the way she wants to keep it. The Tories' ideal family has become a prison for disciplining the working class.

In 1985 Thatcher appealed in the Queen's Speech for a strengthening of 'our traditional sources of discipline and authority'—the family, the church and the school. The Tories want to use the family as a sort of police task force to control the working class. The government has emphasised that parents must play a role in regimenting wayward youth, and take responsibility for 'the anti-social behaviour of their children'. The state has lent a hand by adjusting its myriad youth training schemes and its miserable social security system to keep young people on a tight leash.

Thatcher has encouraged the family to take over many of the functions of the crumbling welfare system. In her view, dependence on the state has cosseted the post-war family and undermined its traditional self-reliance. In a scathing attack on the 'nanny state', Thatcher has emphasised that people have a responsibility to look after themselves. 'I think we've been through a period where too many people have been given to understand that if they have a problem, it's the government's job to cope with it. "I have a problem,

I'll get a grant." "I'm homeless, the government must house me." It's our duty to look after ourselves and then, also, to look after our neighbour' (*Woman's Own,* 31 October 1987).

The true meaning of Thatcher's advocacy of self-help became clear much earlier in her term of office. In documents leaked to the press in 1983, the Family Policy Group (a cabinet think-tank nicknamed the 'Family Patrol Group') revealed the Tories' plans for 'encouraging families to re-assume responsibility' for members in need of special care. The proposals advocated persuading mothers to stay at home to look after pre-school children, the elderly, the chronically sick and the disabled. Thatcher's top advisers outlined a programme for dismantling the welfare state, but presented it as a crusade to promote individual self-reliance and responsibility.

Five years ago the idea that the individual rather than society should be responsible for running comprehensive welfare services was merely wishful thinking on the part of Tory right wingers. Today the responsible family carries the burden for cuts in the health service, social security, education and local authority services.

Victims of Victorian values

The main victims of the drive to restore family values are women. Women carry the burden of increased work in the home resulting from the rundown of the welfare state, as well as the stresses and strains of coping with jobless husbands and making ends meet. A heavier workload in the home makes it more difficult for women to get out to work and play a full part in the wider life of society. Limited access to contraception and abortion reduces women's freedom to escape from the drudgery of domestic work.

Women carry the burden of the cares of holding the family together under the pressures of recession. These pressures often make them the victims of domestic violence and family breakdown. As heads of one-parent families, women are in an even more difficult position. More and more, they are also targets of public prejudice. Debates about infertility and the use of reproductive technology celebrate the virtues of motherhood. Involuntary childlessness is seen as a tragedy. Voluntary childlessness is seen as a perversity. Debates about abortion and promiscuity encourage intolerance against women who fail to conform to the maternal ideal.

The re-assertion of family values is also a threat to lesbians and gay men. The Aids panic has targeted homosexuals as the source of disease and death. It has encouraged a reaction against the more

**Image and reality: Tory austerity
policies are making women's lives
more miserable, and making it harder
to conform to the maternal ideal**

liberal attitudes to homosexuality which emerged in the sixties and seventies, and has served to increase prejudice against lesbians and gay men. The standard-bearers of the official morality elevate the family as sacrosanct and label as deviant all alternatives to marriage and monogamy. Because homosexuality, by its very nature, threatens the family it must be suppressed. This is why the attack on lesbian and gay rights has intensified along with the wider revival of family values.

The oppression of homosexuals undermines the unity and cohesion of the whole working class. It creates suspicion and hostility among workers and helps the establishment to impose its standards of conformity. It reinforces preoccupations about succeeding in heterosexual relationships and family life, and undermines attempts to organise collective organisation and collective activity. Hatred of homosexuals is invariably linked to chauvinist attitudes towards women.

The new morality has created a climate in which conformity is respectable and experimentation a crime. The whole working class stands to suffer the consequences. If the sponsors of the new morality succeed in spreading their prejudices, they will have created the conditions for more law and order measures against the working class. Unless we can counter this offensive by fostering a climate of openness and experimentation, it will become more and more difficult to popularise a radical alternative to establishment ideas.

The post-permissive society

At a time when crisis and conflict are undermining the establishment's ability to keep control, the ideas of the moral rearmers have gained a hearing. Digby Anderson, the director of the Social Affairs Unit, explained the rationale behind the revival of moral orthodoxy:

'It is clear that a society less ordered by political control must seek its order in shared values articulated and transmitted through the family, the neighbourhood, the church and other institutions between the individual and the state, if it is to avoid chaos, crime and despair.' (*The Times,* 28 October 1987)

Anderson appreciates that some sort of moral regeneration is necessary to guard against social breakdown in a period of growing class conflict. The new moralists are keen to assert the traditional values of chastity, marriage, cleanliness, motherhood, community, deference and Christianity against what they call the 'de-moralisation' of modern society.

In the past, according to the gospel of the Digby Anderson school, social cohesion depended on values, sentiments and mores which were common throughout society. This idealised social order has long since passed away, argue the new moralists, to be replaced by a social system in which the old morals have less and less purchase. Writing in the *Salisbury Review,* house-journal of the new right, Oxford professor Bryan Wilson mourned the disappearance of the old taboos:

'To eliminate those prohibitions is an act of de-moralisation—and we have seen many such changes: the legalisation of abortion and homosexuality; the new openness about things once thought pornographic; the abandonment of suicide as a criminal offence; the scaling down of treachery into the more technical offence of revealing official secrets; the fall into virtual desuetude of laws against blasphemy and sacrilege. The old moral prohibitions are superseded. Their latent function, as a community's moral defence, was to reinforce social cohesion: that function is no longer fulfilled in the way it once was.' (October 1985)

Wilson would like to return to the sort of society where everybody knew their place, and what was 'right' and 'wrong' too.

For the new moralists the family is the most important bulwark of the capitalist way of life. Margaret Thatcher believes that 'a nation of free people will only continue to be great if family life continues and the structure of that nation is a family one' (*Woman's Own,* 31 October 1987). Ferdinand Mount, who was the leading force in Thatcher's Family Policy Group, believes that the family is the very foundation of freedom. In his influential book, *The Subversive Family: An Alternative History of Love and Marriage* (1982), Mount declares that the right and proper family form is a heterosexual union, sanctioned by marriage and nourished by children and grandchildren.

The philosophers of the right blame the permissive society for the decline of traditional morality. They regard the disintegration of the family, which they assert to be the outcome of the 'sexual revolution' of the sixties, as a threat to the social order. Roger Scruton, another leading voice of reaction, regards sexual licence not merely as 'an assault on the self', but more importantly, as 'an assault on the social order which produced the self'. Scruton's concern for the survival of the capitalist system and the central institution which helps to keep it going leads him to view promiscuity and homosexuality as inherently immoral:

'The first [promiscuity] destroys the sacral character of the body, and therefore loosens the connection between desire and love. The second [homosexuality] severs desire from its generative tendency.' (*Salisbury Review,* July 1985)

Scruton opposes all sexual activity unless it is put to the service of love and procreation, both within the bounds of marriage. He is particularly opposed to homosexuality because, not only does it separate sex and procreation, it also opens the way to a new promiscuity, 'one which rampages through the barriers of shame':

> 'Unsubdued by the awesome mystery of another sex, driven always to unite with flesh of his own all-too-familiar kind, the homosexual has no use for hesitation, except that which society imposes. He knows with too great a certainty, too great a familiarity, what his partner feels, and has no need for the tiresome stratagems of courtesy, courtship and shame. The gateway to desire, which hides its course in mystery, and diverts it to the path of love, has been burst open, and a short path to pleasure revealed.' (*Salisbury Review,* July 1985)

Scruton is too hung-up even to contemplate the evils of a lesbian relationship, but no doubt he considers this equally abhorrent. His concern is to shroud the sexual act in the veil of secrecy, preach the rectitude of suppressing carnal desires (indeed to declare that some desires *'ought not to exist'*) and perpetuate ignorance and prejudice.

The morality which justifies the present organisation of society depends on mystifying sexual and social relationships. In the reams written about lesbians and gays by the new moralists there is no attempt to offer a rational explanation of homosexuality. Indeed taking in their exhaustive treatment of the subject, the reader is left with the impression that homosexuality was invented in the sixties. In a tirade against gay men, Roy Kerridge talks about homosexuality as if it is a fashion:

> 'First of all there were communists whose transformation into supermen began when they joined the Party. Disillusion followed, so next came hippies, whose transfiguration could be achieved...by swallowing LSD. Alas, the Golden Dawn rapidly became a night of hallucinatory terror. Quickly the universities provided the answer—the new race who would save the world would be lesbians and gays.' ('Predatory Homosexuals', in the *Spectator,* 8 August 1987)

For Kerridge homosexuality is merely the most enduring fad of the permissive society. In the classic manner of the anti-permissive moralist, Kerridge manages to attribute all sorts of deviancy to the same source. In similar fashion Auberon Waugh blames the 'new generation of go-getting, liberated career women' for forcing modern men to embrace 'the homosexual parallel culture in their droves' (*Spectator,* 21 February 1987). The idea that having an orientation to somebody of the same sex might be the natural inclination of large numbers of people is anathema to the philosophers of the new right. For them heterosexuality is the pivot of a morality which embraces only marriage and monogamy.

The moral rearmers blame the decline of British civilisation on the promiscuity of its people. There appears to be no end to the horrors that are now commonly attributed to the permissive society. In his Disraeli lecture in November 1985 Norman Tebbit argued that 'the trigger of today's outburst of crime and violence' lies in 'the era of attitudes of post-war funk which gave birth to the "permissive society" which in turn generated today's violent society'. He provided a detailed catalogue of the crimes of permissiveness:

'The permissives scorned traditional standards. Bad art was as good as good art. Grammar and spelling were no longer important. To be clean was no better than to be filthy. Good manners were no better than bad. Family life was derided as an outdated bourgeois concept. Criminals deserved as much sympathy as their victims. Many homes and classrooms became disorderly—if there was neither right nor wrong there could be no basis for punishment or reward. Violence and soft pornography became accepted in the media.'

Tebbit's targets stretch from the unwashed, unmarried, abstract artist to the bad-mannered media men who cannot spell. Valerie Riches, a leading campaigner for traditional family values, offers another list of the sins of the permissive society:

'A cursory glance at the outcome of permissive legislation in the past 20 years leads one to the conclusion that it always leads to the opening of the floodgates and a whole range of new problems. In the semantic revolution the unborn child becomes "the contents of the womb" or "a blob of jelly", abortion "termination of pregnancy", paedophilia "young love", the illegitimate child "a love child" and the homosexual "gay". Thus the unthinkable becomes palatable; everything is relative and nothing normative.' ('The Politics of Responsible Parenthood' in Richard Whitfield (ed), *Families Matter,* 1987)

Scruton goes even further in detailing the devastating consequences of permissiveness. He believes that the de-moralisation of the British populace endangers national security:

'Religious decline and the collapse of family life are the root causes of man's belief that he has only himself to save, and only one life in which to do so. Why sacrifice that life, in defence of an order whose only meaning lies in its capacity to provide the pap of welfare? Why not abandon national loyalty, if our enemies still offer us the nationalised breast?' (*Salisbury Review,* April 1987)

According to the logic of the new right, permissiveness leads to promiscuity, promiscuity to family breakdown, family breakdown to the demise of patriotism, the demise of patriotism to national disaster. All this makes sense only from the standpoint of a Conservative who understands that adherence to the family and the nation undermines the ability of the working class to pursue its own independent interests.

To rescue the British people from the scourge of de-moralisation the philosophers of the new right propose a good dose of reaction. The moralists know that their case cannot be sustained by logic. Hence they are forced to present their prejudices as eternal moral principles, preached by priests, argued by philosophers and practised by believers in common sense. In a masterful demonstration of this deceit, Margaret Thatcher spelt out the values she considers timeless:

'I was brought up by a Victorian grandmother. We were taught to work jolly hard. We were taught to prove yourself; we were taught self-reliance; we were taught to live within our income. You were taught that cleanliness was next to Godliness. You were taught self-respect. You were taught always to give a hand to your neighbour. You were taught tremendous pride in your country. All of these things are Victorian values. They are also perennial values.' ('Those Good Old Days by Maggie', *Standard,* 15 April 1983)

There is nothing eternal about Thatcher's ragbag of corner-shop prejudices and provincial civic virtues. Throughout history every ruling elite has fashioned its own moral code to legitimise the prevailing social order and its dominant position in it. The Tory government has merely adapted the ethics of the Victorian era to suit the requirements of the capitalist system in the eighties.

In similar fashion Ferdinand Mount proclaims that the traditional nuclear family is a 'natural' unit which has survived the vicissitudes of the centuries:

'The defenders of the family...assert always the privacy and independence of the family, its biological individuality and its rights to live according to its natural instincts. It is for this reason that, even in societies where male supremacy is officially total, the family asserts its maternal values.' (*The Subversive Family*)

If the family is a product of nature which can survive quite well on its own, why do Mount and his co-thinkers feel compelled to keep telling us how good it is? The truth is that the contemporary family is a *social,* not a natural, institution which plays a vital role for the capitalist class. Its defenders proclaim its universality because they fear its dissolution.

Female chastity is also accorded the status of a timeless principle by the moral rearmers, who view promiscuity as an aberration:

'Female modesty and chastity are not just the products of Victorian morality; they have existed throughout recorded history....Even the most depraved slut...longs to be treated like a lady.' (*Salisbury Review,* April 1987)

The moralists insist that chastity is inherent in the female psyche because they fear the consequences for the family of a more open attitude to sex. This is in accordance with the Victorian view that women are asexual guardians of the nation's morals, who have a particular responsibility to tame the animal sexual urges of men.

The establishment's insistence on tradition and continuity in the sphere of morality betrays its real concern: the preservation of a decaying social system based on exploitation and oppression. Such a regime could not endure for even a week without the cement of morality. The ruling class is vitally interested in imposing its moral philosophy on society and in outlawing as immoral ideas and practices which contradict its ends. It conceals its doctrine of submission in the rhetoric of religion, philosophy, patriotism and common sense.

'We're all moralists now'

'Shall we escape new forms of oppressive social control?' asked Bryan Wilson in the *Salisbury Review* in 1985. Today it is no longer even a matter of debate. Thatcher's moral policemen have come to the conclusion that sermons are no longer enough to hold society together. With economic crisis comes social conflict, and with dissent comes repression. In a pointed polemic against the 'reluctant reactionaries', Digby Anderson spelt out the consequences of the new morality:

'Defining what is right involves defining who is wrong. Defining who is in excludes others who do not meet the definition. Approving this behaviour means disapproving that....If society is to move away from the do-it-yourself morality and a philosophy of life which, in the Bishop of London's words, acknowledges no authority outside the individual and his "fulfilment" to one where there are unnegotiable beliefs and values outside him, then with such beliefs and values will come—no, let's not equivocate—will come *back* certain things currently seen as unpleasant.' (*The Times,* 28 October 1987)

At least Anderson is candid: setting absolute standards leads to persecution. His line is that reaction should soldier on and not try to dodge the consequences:

'When the next General Synod discusses whether to take a firm and clear stand on homosexual acts, this is the pivot of the argument. If it takes such a stand, it will discriminate against homosexuals and make stigma, secrecy and blackmail more likely. That may be bad. It may be unfortunate but necessary. It may be good. But what it is not is optional. With clear stands comes discrimination. Sometimes there is no middle road.' (*The Times,* ibid)

A few years ago Anderson's sentiments might have been dismissed as the ravings of an extremist. But it was a sign of the times that the General Synod of the Church of England did indeed take a stand against homosexuality, and in doing so made 'stigma, secrecy and blackmail' an acknowledged fact.

The biggest success of the Tory regime has been in the battle of ideas over issues of sex and morality. The opposition parties, the labour movement, the churches and even sections of the left have come to accept the establishment view to such an extent that the Tories have won every crucial debate. The new morality is a potent weapon for the establishment because there has been no coherent challenge to the official orthodoxy.

How successful have the Tories been in promoting the new morality? It is undoubtedly the case that they have managed to create an atmosphere of restraint and censorship. There are many signs of a shift in the climate of opinion towards an acceptance of the official prejudices.

The **Labour Party** has moved further and further on to the moral ground occupied by the Tories. Labour leader Neil Kinnock justifies his claim to the title of a respected politician by admitting he is a self-confessed 'reactionary' when it comes to the family. In the run-up to the 1987 general election the Labour leadership made no secret of its hostility to campaigns for lesbian and gay rights. After a disastrous performance in the Greenwich by-election, Kinnock's assistant Patricia Hewitt wrote a letter to Frank Dobson MP, the campaign organiser, blaming Labour's defeat on its association with 'loony left' causes like lesbian and gay rights. The Catholic tabloid, the *Universe,* published an interview in which Kinnock portrayed the Labour Party as a pious institution which the Pope could safely support. Jumping on the Tory bandwagon about sex education in schools, Kinnock declared that nobody 'has the right to teach children that which their parents morally and spiritually disagree with' (6 March 1987). Later in the year the Labour Party lined up behind Tory bigots like Dame Jill Knight MP to support legislation banning the 'promotion of homosexuality' in schools.

The **Church of England** has become more and more embroiled in the debate about morality. The ferment in the church over the issue of homosexuality is an indication of how all sections of the establishment are now being whipped into line behind the crusade to restore conventional values. While stopping short of endorsing the demand that gay clergymen should be expelled from their parishes, the resolution on sexual morality passed at the November Synod of the Church of England revealed the ascendancy of the spirit of Thatcherism over the established church. The subsequent suicide of Dr Gareth Bennett, author of the controversial preface to the latest edition of *Crockford's Clerical Directory,* testified to the bitterness of the battle now being fought between the traditionalists and the liberal establishment over the moral direction of the church. While there may be differences over how far to pursue the anti-homosexual witch-hunt inside the church, both sides are moving towards a more active role in enforcing public morality. Hence, the Archbishop of Canterbury, Dr Robert Runcie, had no compunction about backing the Bishop of Ripon David Young's decision to refuse to ordain practising gays.

The state of **'public opinion'** is harder to gauge. Here we are forced to rely on often dubious media polls which register the Tories' success in selling their panics to the general public. For example, a Mori poll conducted at the end of January 1987, after the first stage of the government's Aids campaign, revealed that Aids had become the fifth most important issue for the British electorate. It was considered more important than education, pensions, defence and foreign policy. There is evidence that the panic about child abuse and the clamour for restrictions on abortion rights have made an impact too. At bus-stops, in shops, at school, in pubs, people talk incessantly about child abuse. Esther Rantzen's *ChildWatch* programme and ChildLine service turned the campaign against child abuse into a national crusade. A chilling indication of the consequences of this sort of panic occurred at the Headmasters' conference in October 1987, where teachers' strikes were denounced as 'a form of child abuse' which should be made illegal. Abortion has not acquired the same prominence in public debate. But a succession of parliamentary bills to restrict abortion rights and effective campaigns by the anti-abortion groups Spuc and Life have been influential in changing the climate of opinion. A series of polls in 1987 revealed growing support for a reduction in the time-limit for terminations.

The outlook of Britain's **youth** on moral issues is a key register of the Tories' success. Various surveys seem to show that here too the official view of morality has made its mark. But the results also reveal an ambivalent response to Tory moralising that is probably shared by much wider sections of society. The McCann-Erickson *Youth Study* was carried out in 1986 and 1987, and addressed two generations of young people: the 'Baby Boomers' (aged 20-25 years) and the 'New Wave' young (aged 15-19 years). 'When asked questions on aspects of social and sexual morality,' noted the

**Britain's youth are not immune to
Tory moralising, but nor have they
fallen for Thatcher's Victorian values**

authors, 'the young gave highly conventional answers.' Indeed they observed 'some reinforcement of traditional attitudes, some reduction of tolerance even, over attitudes in 1977'. Sex outside marriage was seen as wrong by a third of the respondents, and being unfaithful was almost universally condemned. According to the report considerably more young people than 10 years ago disapprove of divorce, drug abuse, drinking and homosexuality. Asked if they might indulge in some of the activities they considered immoral, however, considerable numbers stated that perhaps they would (with the notable exception of having a homosexual relationship). Most young people saw Aids as 'a problem that "they" should do something about, rather than something to be worried about personally'. Only 17 per cent worried 'a lot' about getting Aids, with a third more worrying 'a little'.

The same ambivalence has characterised the response of **left-wing radicals** and **feminists** to the Tories' re-assertion of moral orthodoxy. The radical response to Thatcher's elevation of the family has generally been to offer a critique of the hypocrisy of a government which glorifies the family at the same time as it attacks it through cuts in benefits and services. Some feminists have retreated further, and have come to extol the joys of motherhood and family life. On Aids the gay movement and the left have largely accepted the government's safe sex campaign at face value, choosing to ignore its anti-homosexual message. 'Too little, too late' has been the response to a state-sponsored crusade to enforce sexual conformity. The radical response to the child abuse panic has combined an acceptance of dubious claims of a vast increase in abuse with an attack on the Tories for exacerbating the problem by slashing social services. The well-worn left-wing observation that child abuse 'has always been with us' is incapable of challenging the motives behind the establishment crusade. The Tories' opponents have rallied their diminished forces to defend abortion rights, but they have proved no match for the vocal pro-life groups. The women's movement and the left have lowered their horizons to a defence of the 1967 Abortion Act, a piece of legislation that negates the very idea of abortion on demand.

Stop the strong-arm state

The Tories' success in establishing common ground with their opponents on moral issues has had important consequences. While active enthusiasm for reaction remains confined to a minority, the authorities can rely on a wider consensus of passive support. The lack of a coherent alternative to the new moralists means that the establishment has a free rein to mobilise public opinion behind its repressive programme. The Tories' real triumph has thus been in fostering a climate of public opinion which is sympathetic towards more moral state intervention. A fictional account of the state of the nation as it enters the nineties published in a Sunday newspaper reveals an acute perception of the likely outcome of the new moralism:

'He switched on the radio in time to catch "Yesterday in Parliament" and the scenes of uproar that attended the final reading of the Sexually Transmitted Diseases Bill (1989), which the day before had passed its final reading by only 10 votes. It had been a free vote, the first since capital punishment had been restored a year ago, and the result enabled draconian measures to be taken to contain the relentless and apparently unmeasurable spread of Aids.

'Tests were already required before the issue of a marriage licence, and were routinely made, with or without consent or knowledge, and without proper legal backing, when a patient entered hospital. Most employers had private requirements for job applicants to prove a clean bill of health....Now it would be a card-carrying matter.' (*Observer* magazine, 29 November 1987)

The detail may be far-fetched, but the flavour of repression is convincing. Incidences of state interference which would have been greeted with outrage a few years ago are now accepted without a fuss.

● **Homosexuality**
In December 1987 Tory backbenchers, supported by the Labour Party, proposed a new clampdown on lesbian and gay rights. They put forward an amendment to the Local Government Bill banning 'the promotion of homosexuality' in schools, and the funding of organisations that promote homosexuality. If the bill becomes law in its amended form it will be a step backwards towards the further criminalisation of homosexuality. It will give the courts powers to take action against councils or schools found guilty of associating with the cause of homosexual rights.

● **Child abuse**
In December 1987 leading barrister Louis Blom-Cooper recommended tough new powers for police and social workers to intervene in families where child abuse is suspected. His comments came in his report on the inquiry into the death of four-year old Kimberly Carlile, who was starved, beaten and tortured to death in June 1986

by her stepfather. The panic about child abuse has become the pretext for granting draconian powers to state agencies.

● **Abortion rights**
In October 1987 Liberal MP David Alton introduced his private member's bill, aimed at enforcing new controls on abortion, to parliament. It is expected that Alton's bid to reduce the legal time-limit for terminations from 28 to 18 weeks will be amended to set the limit at around 24 weeks. If it becomes law, whatever date the politicians agree on, the bill will hand even more control to the state and the medical establishment to regulate women's lives.

● **Sterilisation**
In May 1987 the law lords ruled in favour of sterilising Jeanette, a mentally handicapped girl. They considered it legitimate for the courts to remove the 'basic right' of a woman to conceive and give birth because Jeanette was incapable of informed consent to sexual intercourse or marriage. Many people regarded the judgement as humane and sensible. But the case opened the way for the courts to have a say in who should and should not be allowed to have children, and for the state to step up its interference in matters of sex and reproduction.

● **Censorship**
In September 1987 home secretary Douglas Hurd declared the need to stop Britain's 'descent into slovenliness' in response to an outcry about sex and violence on television. The immediate cause of the controversy was ITV's decision to broadcast the Joan Collins show, *Sins,* before 9pm on a Sunday night. The tabloids, Tory MPs and 'outraged viewers' like Mary Whitehouse raised a storm of protest about the scenes of 'appalling sadism'. The broadcasting authorities launched an inquiry, ITV agreed to establish a tighter previewing system, and Hurd outlined plans for a new television watchdog committee. Effectively this means giving Mary Whitehouse the official go-ahead to dictate what we can and cannot watch. The fact that Mary Whitehouse's views on Joan Collins can now start a national debate, leading to a new system of home office censorship, is a sign of the times.

These are only a few examples of the forward march of the moral policemen. Unless we take a stand now, the *Observer* scenario may soon be here. The growth of reaction is preparing the way for the drastic measures the capitalists need to impose to resolve the crisis of their system. Unless the new morality is challenged it will have a divisive and demoralising effect on our ability to organise resistance to the system.

The class struggle is not simply about going on strike and standing on picket lines. It is a contest of conflicting ideas. The question of whose view of the world will prevail confronts us every day. We have to extend the struggle against their system into the moral sphere too. Our task is to challenge the apostles of reaction on their own terrain and spread contempt for official morality.

Den and Angie's on-off relationship has captivated the nation and kept *EastEnders* at the top of the ratings league

2.
Policing the family

Will Den and Angie make it? Will Billy and Doreen get back together again? Will Des and Daphne stick it out? Will this *Blind Date* lead to wedded bliss? Could Chas and Di split up? Is Fergie really pregnant? And will Edward ever find a steady girlfriend? These are the questions which are meant to exercise the minds of the nation. The focus on the family at all levels of popular culture from soap operas to game shows to the royal family confirms its central place in modern life.

There is a remarkable consensus of support for the family in British society. 'In their attitudes towards marriage and other family matters,' concluded the *British Social Attitudes* report in October 1987, 'the British emerge as highly and consistently conventional.' The typical household consists of a breadwinner father, a homemaker mother and two children. Two thirds of the people interviewed for the survey supported the notion that 'as a society we ought to do more to safeguard the institution of marriage.'

The concept of the ideal marriage has changed considerably over the past 40 years. In the *Matrimonial Survey* of 1947 a happy marriage was defined as a complementary relationship, with 'man as breadwinner and defender of the home, woman as housewife and mother; man as aggressive and woman as timid'. By 1969, when the survey was repeated, a more common view of marriage was one where the partners should have more equal roles. The complementary marriage was being replaced by a companionate one, with the emphasis now on compatibility and friendship between husband and wife. The 1987 *Social Attitudes* report confirmed the trend towards the companionate partnership, within a conventional framework. The view of an ideal marriage included sharing a wide range of decisions from money management to planning a family.

Ninety per cent of the British population pursue the ideal of marriage and family life. Despite the marked decline in religious observance some 60 per cent of marriages still take place in church. About four fifths of British people live in households headed by a married couple and three quarters of these contain children. Marriage is as popular as ever among young women. Sales of *Bride* magazine and *Prima* (the new and highest-selling monthly dedicated to feminine virtues) are booming. 'The family based on the married couple and their children with a commitment to permanence,' observed the Social Affairs Unit, 'is still the statistical and moral norm' (*Family Portraits,* 1986). For the vast majority of people the family is at the centre of their life in society.

For many people the family is a refuge from the grind of work, a source of comfort and enjoyment in a harsh world. But to judge by the reams written and volumes spoken about the family today—by politicians, church leaders, media pundits, education experts, royalty—anybody would think it was an endangered species.

Politicians of all parties proclaim their commitment to family life and promote their policies to appeal to the mythical average family. The sanctity of family life, and women's role at the centre of it, has been an enduring theme of Conservative propaganda, and never more than in the Thatcher era. The central message of Thatcher's first general election rally in May 1987 was the need to defend and encourage the family: 'Isn't it moral that people should want to improve the material standard of living of their families by their own effort? Isn't it moral that families should work for the means to look after their old folks? Isn't it moral that people should save, so as to be responsible for themselves?' (cited in *the next step,* 22 May 1987). The Labour Party too has staked a claim to be the party of the family. Back in 1977 Labour leader James Callaghan declared his government's commitment to 'strengthen the stability and quality of family life in Britain'. Out of office in the eighties, Labour leader Neil Kinnock has pursued the same theme, parading Glenys and the kids to show that he is a committed family man.

According to the church authorities marriages are made in heaven and made to last. The Church of England Synod in November 1987 stressed the validity of 'biblical and traditional teaching on chastity and fidelity in personal relationships'. It insisted that sexual intercourse should take place only 'within a permanent married relationship', and condemned 'fornication and adultery' and 'homosexual genital acts'. The teaching of the Catholic Church is even more prohibitive. A recent Vatican document provided some answers to questions confronting Roman Catholics: the answer was invariably *no*. The document branded as immoral test-tube fertilisation, surrogate motherhood, sex selection, artificial insemination, contraception, abortion, masturbation and embryo experimentation. Sexual intercourse is permissible only within marriage, and then only when it is an expression of love and an attempt to create a new life ('Instruction on Respect for Human Life in Its Origins and the Dignity of Procreation: Answers to Some Questions Today', March 1987).

The churches are aghast at the trend towards marital breakdown and the ready recourse to the divorce courts. The Right Reverend Stanley Booth-Clibborn, the Bishop of Manchester, spoke out against young people who, he reckons, make little effort to sustain their marriages. 'In years gone by husbands and wives kept things going in spite of the strains of family life. When things go wrong these days the tendency is for couples to break up and head for the divorce courts' (*Daily Mirror,* 28 August 1987). The priests' advice to the faithful is to persevere and pray for redemption.

The media is another British institution which is preoccupied by the family. 'A family is a thing we carry inside us,' declared journalist Andrew Brown in the *Independent* last year, 'it is our frame for the world.' The family certainly seems to be the framework into which the press and television fit the news. The pregnancy of *TV-am* star Anne Diamond last year became the pretext for a daily dose of the joys of motherhood in the tabloid press, until we were finally presented with the bundle of joy itself on breakfast television. Fergie's valiant struggle to conceive after eight years on the pill captivated the gossip columnists and royal family watchers until she finally triumphed early in 1988; the royal pregnancy then took over the feature pages and the news bulletins.

Public debates about infertility and the new reproductive technology have served to reinforce the centrality of parenthood. The media have celebrated breakthroughs in fertility drugs and test-tube babies as major achievements in allowing every woman to reach fulfilment through childbirth. The press has an apparently insatiable appetite for anything to do with mothers and babies. When the Waltons of Liverpool became the first British family to have surviving sextuplets, Mrs Walton gave birth to an even bigger business in marketing multiple babies.

Ever since the publication of the board of education's 'Sex Education in Schools and Youth Organisations' in 1943, the education system has been geared to training young people to become responsible parents. Last September a department of education circular to every school in Britain declared that sex education 'should be set within a clear, moral framework in which pupils are helped to appreciate the benefits of stable family life, and to recognise the physical and emotional risks of casual and promiscuous behaviour'. It went on to insist that 'there is no place in any school in any circumstances for teaching which advocates homosexual behaviour, which presents it as the "norm", or which encourages homosexual experimentation by pupils.' Indeed, warned the circular, 'encouraging or procuring homosexual acts by pupils who are under the age of consent is a criminal offence.'

The proposed Clause 28 of the Local Government Bill aims to enforce the proscription of any mention of homosexuality in schools by law. Indeed it goes far beyond the bounds of the classroom by banning local authorities from 'promoting homosexuality' in general. The controversy about schools promoting 'positive images' of lesbians and gays, or 'spreading filth on the rates' as Dame Jill Knight put it, has been accompanied by accusations that the education system does little to prepare pupils for the problems of parenthood. In July 1987 the Professional Association of Teachers called for greater priority to be given in the school curriculum to training young people for family life: 'This neglect of training for parenthood in our schools explains a great many evils of our society and is something which ought to give the teaching profession and others sleepless nights' (*Independent, 28 July 1987*). If the Tories get their way schoolchildren might not have any books to read after the government's great education reform, but at least they'll know all about the family.

Since Victorian times the royal family has been held up as an example to the populace. 'We have come to regard the Crown as the head of our morality,' wrote the great constitutional authority Walter Bagehot. This was no mean feat on Queen Victoria's part, given royalty's well-established reputation for debauchery and decadence. Both Edward VII and George II were notorious for their philandering. Today the royals are supposed to set an example, though marital strife—the Snowdon divorce, the tensions between Anne and Mark—is not unknown. However, the wedding of Charles and Diana in 1981 and the swift arrival of William and Harry provided the national role model. Now that Charles and Diana seem to have run into a marital rift, the papers are full of advice about what the royal couple should do. Still, it shows they're human.

What's so special about the family?

Why are the British so obsessed with the family? Why does the absurdly anachronistic royal family still exist? In fact the royals provide the clearest illustration of why the establishment is so keen to promote the family. The middle class family is based on the preservation of private property. For the rich, the famous and royalty, the central aim of monogamous marriage is to make the man supreme in the family and to propagate, as the future heirs to his wealth and titles, children who are indisputably his own. The royal family keeps up the image of marital fidelity because of the continued importance of inheriting titles and property. One reason why it took Charles so long to get married was his difficulty in finding himself a virgin of the required stock. The rules of monogamy ensure that the children of the royal marriage belong to the husband. Diana still stands to be executed or exiled if she commits adultery. The children bear their father's name and inherit his worldly goods, as well as his claim to the throne. This arrangement guarantees that the propertied classes survive generation after generation. As long as the succession to the throne and the inheritance of property is safeguarded, it matters little if Charles and Diana never see each other from one month to the next.

There is no such rationale for the working class family. Here there is no property, and hence no apparent need for monogamy and male supremacy. Yet as Norman Tebbit recently observed, working class people appear to be firmer supporters of the family than the upper classes: 'The permissive society was generated in the cocktail bar circuit. Family values are tighter in the working class. Reasonable people don't like being on welfare, they want to work. They want to hand something on to their kids, to own their own home and a few shares' (*Sun,* 5 October 1987). For working class people economic, social and personal considerations are decisive in determining the pattern of family life. Most working class people have no other way of surviving in society and bringing up children than in the family.

The family provides a place to eat and sleep, some rest and recreation from the grind of working life, and some support in times of illness, disability and old age. For the majority of people their family is their only comfort. It is not surprising that marriage and family life remain so popular.

The family provides a framework for maintaining and reproducing the working class, day in day out, week in week out, year after year, generation after generation. The modern family unit is founded on the domestic slavery of women. Women carry the main burden of keeping the family together, as the child-bearers and chief child-rearers, cooks, cleaners, nurses and providers of general household services. The capitalist class gets these services free of charge. This is why it is state policy to encourage marriage and having children, and why contraception and abortion are restricted. The family curtails women's freedom and confines relationships between people to those which are acceptable to the system.

The family also performs an important stabilising function. In a private letter written during the 1987 general election campaign Thatcher explained that the task of safeguarding the family had assumed even more importance in the Britain of the late eighties:

'Marriage and the family are two of the most important institutions on which society is based. Particularly at this time of rapid social change and accompanying stresses, marriage has never been more important in preserving a stable and responsible society.' (Cited in Richard Whitfield (ed), *Families Matter,* 1987)

Thatcher hopes that by encouraging people to focus on family life and by emphasising individual preoccupations she can reduce the risk of the working class turning to collective solutions to its problems. Modern society is composed of millions of individual families. The family stabilises society by fragmenting potential resistance to the system. This is why the establishment defines alternatives to family life as illegal, immoral or uneconomic.

Family law

It is a paradox yet to be explained by the defenders of the family why the institution, which they insist is natural, should need to be regulated by such a formidable array of laws and customs. On the one hand, the family is presented as an essentially private, self-sufficient body. On the other hand, it is subject to a wide range of public and intrusive regulations.

Right-wing moralists condemn the legal system for not doing enough to sustain families, and denounce the divorce laws for breaking them up. The Divorce Law Reform Act of 1969 (consolidated in the Matrimonial Causes Act, 1973) allowed divorce after a separation of three years where both partners agreed, and after five years where one partner disagreed. Since 1984 a petition for divorce can be presented after one year. Paradoxically, however, the whole aim of allowing divorce is to safeguard the institution of marriage. According to the Law Commission the 1969 Act aimed to '*buttress* rather than undermine the stability of marriage and when regrettably a marriage has broken down, to enable the empty legal shell to be destroyed with the maximum fairness and the minimum bitterness, distress and humiliation' ('Reform of the Grounds of Divorce: The Field of Choice', HMSO, 1967). The preamble to the 1969 law describes it as 'an act to...facilitate reconciliation in matrimonial causes.'

The objective of attempting to reconcile the estranged parties was fundamental to the whole concept of divorce reform. The state took the pragmatic view that it was more sensible to allow people to extricate themselves from failed marriages, if only to enable the irreconcilable pair to start all over again with new partners. For the majority of couples who split up, divorce is merely the transitional stage to a second marriage.

The sanctity of the marriage contract, as well as its legal status, restricts access to the wife's sexual and reproductive functions to the husband alone. The rules of monogamy guarantee that the children of the marriage belong to the husband. The law does not recognise rape in marriage. The Sexual Offences Act of 1956 states that 'a man cannot as a rule be guilty as a principal in the first degree of rape upon his wife, for the consent to marital intercourse impliedly given in the contract of matrimony cannot in general be retracted.' In January 1988 a bench of magistrates in Gwent acquitted a man who raped and tortured his wife when she threatened to leave him by declaring that he was 'only trying to save his marriage' (*Daily Mirror,* 13 January 1988). The law also states that where husband and wife are separated, even if they are not legally divorced, this revokes the consent given at the time of marriage. In December 1987, however, Mr Justice Jupp made up his own law when he freed a man who raped his former wife: 'I do not regard this as what the public often thinks of as rape. It is rape, but a rare sort of rape. This is within the family and does not impinge on the public' (*Daily Mirror,* 16 December 1987). According to this judgement the marriage contract implies consent to perpetual rape even after the union has been legally dissolved.

The inadequacy of contraception makes it easy for women to become pregnant. But the law makes it difficult for women to terminate an unwanted pregnancy, thus pushing women towards marriage and motherhood. The 1967 Abortion Act allows a woman to have an abortion only if she can get the permission of two doctors; in many areas she will also need around £100 to pay to have it done in a private clinic. It is very difficult to get an abortion on the NHS after 12 weeks anywhere in Britain, and in some places it is virtually impossible to get an NHS abortion at any stage in pregnancy. Countless women are denied the right to terminate a pregnancy by anti-abortion doctors or simply because of cuts in abortion services. Persistent attempts to amend the 1967 Abortion Act and strident anti-abortion organisations have created a climate of prejudice against women seeking abortions. The present abortion law restricts women's opportunities to pursue activities outside of family life.

A fundamental premise of family life is that parents, especially mothers, rather than the state, must take responsibility for rearing children. The legal doctrine of 'parens patriae' holds that the state should intervene in family life in the manner of a judicious parent. The state thus takes on a surveillance role, interfering only when things go wrong. The 1929 Infant Life (Preservation) Act amended the law on abortion and infanticide. The 1938 Infanticide Act made a woman who causes the death of her child under the age of 12 months guilty of a felony. The 1908 Incest Act was the first official recognition of child sexual abuse within the family. It has since been supplemented by further legislation. For example, the 1978 Protection of Children Act makes it an offence to take, distribute, exhibit or advertise indecent photographs of children. In July 1987 the home office announced that the maximum penalty for parents who wilfully neglect their children would be increased from a two-year to a 10-year prison sentence under a new clause in the Criminal Justice Bill. The continuing panic about child abuse may well lead to more repressive legislation.

Numerous other laws surround the family with legal protections. Two worth noting are the 1967 Sexual Offences Act and the 1985 Surrogacy Arrangements Act. The first forbids young men to engage in homosexual relations before the age of 21, closing down the alternatives to heterosexual relationships and marriage. The second prohibits commercial agencies from engaging women to act as surrogate mothers and penalises the advertisement of surrogacy services, thus curtailing an activity which the authorities considered could undermine motherhood and bring the family into disrepute.

The government is presently debating further legal controls on surrogate motherhood. The mounting wave of prejudice against lesbians and gays is likely to lead to even further prohibitions against homosexuality. The legal framework that sustains the family confirms that it is a social institution, not a natural creation.

Family morals

Official morality backs up the law. Conventional morality combines both a positive promotion of the ideal family and a negative proscription of all departures from the norm. We are taught that love means marriage and sex means children. From the onset of puberty the pressure is on to find a partner, settle down and prepare for parenthood. Popular wisdom has it that there is something wrong with people who don't get married. Society patronises or shuns those who do not conform to the ideal: spinsters and bachelors are the objects of sympathy or suspicion, homosexuals are treated with contempt, people feel sorry for single parents, and regard celibacy as just peculiar.

We have seen how the forces of the establishment have gone on the offensive to promote family life. With equal determination they have manned the barricades against any threat to the family.

Restrictions on sexual behaviour play an important role in legitimising the family. The authorities have sponsored a series of moral panics to deter people from sexual activity and experimentation outside the bounds of marriage. Those who refuse to stick to the sexual straight and narrow will suffer the consequences. Condoms have been openly advertised and made readily available for the first time as part of the Aids panic—as a means of preventing disease, not for preventing pregnancy. Women who take the pill are said to be promiscuous, and have only themselves to blame if they end up with cervical cancer. Promiscuity is also blamed for causing infertility, itself a focus of public concern as a barrier to women's ultimate fulfilment. Women who have abortions are condemned for murdering sentient fetuses. The aim of the official morality is to channel everybody's desire for sexual and emotional gratification into a commitment to marriage and the family.

The establishment is ruthless in its treatment of those who breach its moral prerogatives. The state turns gay men into criminals because their sex lives do not fit in with the family framework: more than 2000 men are arrested every year for the 'sex crimes' of homosexual behaviour. Any public display of sexuality by lesbians and gays—from holding hands to a kiss—is liable to land them in a police cell. In April 1987 the trailer for the film *Prick Up Your Ears*, based on the life of gay playwright Joe Orton, was censored on the grounds that the word 'homosexual' was considered unfit for public consumption. The Aids panic has unleashed a wave of attacks on homosexuals. The Gay London Policing Group recorded a quadruple increase in attacks on gay men in the capital in 1987. Just before Christmas bigots fire-bombed the offices of the London-based newspaper *Capital Gay*, exactly a year after police arrested 12 members of the Lesbian and Gay Youth Movement in Wombourne for protesting outside the home of a Tory councillor who suggested gassing gays as a cure for Aids.

Given the strength of prejudice against those who deviate from the prescribed sexual and social norms it is not surprising that so few people escape from marriage and conventional family life.

Family economics

If all else fails economic realism will push people into families. Women's lack of economic independence, enforced through discrimination in the job market and institutionalised through the social security system, makes them dependent on men and the family for survival.

Women are trapped in a vicious circle. Women are second class citizens in the labour market because of their role as carers in the home. Women are forced into the family because their inferior position in the world of work means they cannot survive outside it. The fact that most mothers are married means that the state does not expect that their own wages should be enough to sustain them. Women are confined to the margins of the economy, concentrated in relatively few occupations, frequently those with a large demand for part-time labour, offering low pay and poor conditions. In 1986, 42 per cent of full-time women workers were employed in clerical and related occupations, and 19 per cent in education, health and welfare. Women working part-time are concentrated in catering, cleaning, hairdressing and other personal service occupations.

Today nearly half of all female employees work part-time. Politicians and businessmen often claim that this is 'what she wants'. In reality it is what *they* want. Part-time work means a cheap, flexible labour force that can be employed when the bosses most need it, while relieving them of the responsibility for paying a living wage.

Some 80 per cent of part-timers are married. But part-time work is also becoming the norm for all women, even if they have no dependants. In 1979 eight per cent of women in the 16-19 age group worked part-time: today 30 per cent of these women are part-timers. The part-time trap affects women who have no children, often because they cannot find anything else. Britain's part-time labour force includes 13 per cent of single, childless working women, 40 per cent of married working women with no dependant children and 70 per cent of working women with dependant children.

Self-employment is another growth area—women now make up 25 per cent of all the self-employed. This does not reflect a boom in woman entrepreneurs opening antique shops and boutiques, but more the fact that women are increasingly forced to work 'on the lump' without any of the legislative and welfare protections of direct employment. There has also been a big increase in temporary working in the public sector and in personal services, two areas where women tend to be concentrated. Temporary workers are normally brought in on the lowest grade, and are offered no chance of advancement. In social security offices, for example, all temporary workers are brought in on the clerical assistant grade, earning £77 a week. Two thirds of Britain's 1.4m temporary workers are women.

The insecure and low-paid nature of female employment exerts strong pressures on working class women to get married. Single women who are dependent on social security, whether or not they have children, are even more likely to look to marriage as a way out of the poverty trap. Today most women find it difficult to get by on the miserable benefits provided by the DHSS. From April 1988 a number of changes proposed in the Tories' new social security legislation will make it almost impossible to survive without working or getting married. Supplementary benefit will no longer take account of individual needs, and special payments for heating, diet or laundry as well as for beds, cookers, maternity wear, baby clothes and equipment will all be abolished. Instead claimants will be lent money from a social fund that will have to be repaid from their weekly benefit.

Claimants will have to pay 20 per cent of their rates on their flat or house. Widows under 45 will no longer be paid a widow's pension. Child benefit, the only independent income many women receive, is no longer raised in line with inflation. The Tories have stopped short of abolishing it outright, but plan to phase it out gradually. Single parents claiming social security now and working part-time are allowed to deduct child-minding expenses before the 'earning rule' applies. This is to be abolished. The £25 maternity grant has already vanished, to be replaced by a means-tested grant of £80 for women on supplementary benefit, which is less than they currently receive. Even the government estimates that equipment for a new baby costs £187: some 500 000 women will get nothing.

Any single woman who claims supplementary benefit immediately comes under the eye of special social security investigators—the sex snoopers. If they can establish that you have a steady relationship with a man, they will take away your right to claim benefit independently. In this way the state can save money—the entitlement for a 'partner' is considerably less than that for a 'householder'. At the same time the state pushes women into dependence on the man, because benefit for both 'partners' is paid directly to him. Every year more than 30 000 women lose their right to claim benefit independently. To prove cohabitation the snoopers are supposed to show that a woman allows the man to stay at her home for three or more consecutive nights.

The social security rule forcing fathers to pay maintenance for their children is another weapon the state uses against women. Like the cohabitation rule this saves the state money, and promotes the notion of family responsibility by making women rely on men to support their children. The 'liable relative' officer checks on the paternity of the children of every single mother who signs on, and makes every effort to track down the man so that the state can get out of providing the woman with the benefit she needs to look after the child.

The whole welfare system works against people who choose to live a different lifestyle. When the family has the law, morality and economics on its side people have little choice but to conform.

Is the family falling apart?

The new moralists proclaim that the family is in peril and that something must be done to arrest its decline if we are to maintain civilisation as we know it. Launching the National Campaign for the Family in October 1987, Richard Whitfield argued that a neglect of 'home defence' had sown the seeds of social collapse:

'Stable and strong families can no longer be taken for granted. They are disintegrating at an alarming rate as the social fabric changes at a faster rate than at any previous stage of recorded history. Yet we cannot have a viable society without them.' (*Families Matter*, 1987)

Victims of the Thatcher years: Val Kestle and her children were left to cope alone after Ian Kestle was jailed fighting for jobs in the 1984-85 miners' strike

Establishment fears for the future of the family reflect the profound sense of moral crisis in the ruling class.

The defenders of the old order marshal masses of statistics to support their theory of family breakdown and national decline. They cite the high divorce rate: one in three marriages are now likely to break up, with about 170 000 divorces going through the courts every year. The rate of divorces has risen by 400 per cent over the past 20 years, and England and Wales now top the European divorce league along with Denmark. About 60 per cent of first-time marriages, and 50 per cent of second marriages, are breaking up. If this trend continues one in five children will come from broken homes. One in seven families are now headed by a lone parent, doubling the number of one-parent families since 1966. Almost one in four babies in England and Wales are now born outside marriage, and the numbers are still rising according to the Office of Population Censuses and Surveys (see *Population Trends* 50, HMSO, 1987). In fact this reflects the national swing to cohabitation rather than a rise in one-parent families, a move confirmed in the official 1988 *Social Trends* report.

The prophets of doom complain of declining birth rates, the availability of contraception and abortion, declining church attendance, the growing acceptance of alternative lifestyles, the rise in dependency on welfare, the explosion of child abuse, the spread of alcohol, solvent and drug abuse and the increase in juvenile crime. They point to the distortion in the concept of the family: it can mean a commune, a homosexual couple, cohabitees, children with single parents. Valerie Riches of the Responsible Society warns of the dangers of this loose terminology:

'The commonly held values and the concept of individual responsibility which have held society together in the past are now seriously undermined. The family is in a state of crisis, as, in consequence, is the rest of society.' (*Families Matter,* 1987)

Yet again the source of the moral contagion is identified in the swinging sixties. Permissiveness is said to have weakened traditional values, leading in turn to the breakdown of the family, and to social strife. In reality the momentum lies in the other direction. The social turmoil resulting from economic crisis has led to a breakdown of the old consensus. In the recession the ideal family model is further and further removed from the reality of family life for most working class people. The pressures on the family resulting from unemployment, falling incomes, growing impoverishment and deteriorating services intensify the stresses and strains of family life. The result is more rows, more domestic violence, more neglect of children, more family breakdowns and higher rates of single parenthood. Yet the more their decaying system destroys working class families, the more insistent are Britain's rulers in proclaiming the virtues of family life.

In March 1987 26-year old Michael Tracey was given a 15-month stretch in prison for 'cruelty and neglect' after his three children died in a fire at home. His tragic case illustrates the double-standards of a system which champions family life, while forcing people to risk their children's lives to survive. Tracey was separated from his wife and struggling to bring up his two sons and a daughter in Kennington, South London. His neighbours and social workers agreed he was a loving father who took a part-time job at a local pub to raise the family income. One day in June 1986 he could not get a baby-sitter to cover his lunchtime shift. So he shut the children in a bedroom and went to work. When he returned they were dead, killed by fumes from a fire they started with matches and disposable nappies. Tracey's story shows up the barbarism of a system that forces people to spend most of their day working for an employer to earn a living, to spend the rest of it looking after children without assistance, and to live their own lives in the moments in between. When something goes wrong, they receive a stern lecture from an upper class twit in a wig and end up in jail.

In July 1987 Thomas Corlett appeared in court accused of the murder of his wife Erika. In December 1985 Corlett had strangled his wife 'because' she put the mustard on the left side of his place instead of the right. 'It was not the placing of the mustard,' explained Corlett, 'it was the way it was done' (*Daily Mirror,* 10 July 1987). In that year 100 wives were killed by their husbands and 15 husbands were killed by their wives.

Behind the recorded incidents in which domestic tensions erupted into events which seized the headlines lies a mass of unrecorded suffering, injury and illness. Given the intense strains of family life what is surprising is that there is not *more* divorce, infidelity, violence and murder. Most couples learn to live with each other's irritating habits. Most people put up with their sexual problems. Most parents learn to cope with their tiresome children. Most families make do with not enough money. Most men and women who get married soon discover that capitalism makes its ideal of marital bliss impossible to achieve. Yet most working class people hold on to their families because nobody has offered them anything better.

Problem families

The propagandists of the ruling class are prepared to stir up all sorts of prejudices to keep the family going. Yet the tendency towards more overt state interference in family life threatens to land the establishment in even more of a mess. The crusade to bolster the family works for and against the authorities. On the one hand it encourages individuals to try to conform to the expected standards of family behaviour, and fosters an acceptance of more regulation by the state. On the other hand state interference exposes problems that could bring the family into disrepute, and stirs up conflict in the private sphere of family life.

The panic about child abuse is the best example of the double-edged character of the state's attempt to police the family. The child abuse scandal has been successful in focusing attention on the family and its problems, and in creating a climate of public opinion supportive of more state intervention. But the constant focus on child abuse also encourages people to question a system that drives families to murder their children, and the increasingly repressive activities of the authorities risk provoking a backlash.

Jasmine Beckford, Tyra Henry, Heidi Koseda and Kimberly Carlile have become household names. Jasmine Beckford was battered to death by her father in July 1984. Tyra Henry was beaten and bitten to death by her father in August 1984. Heidi Koseda was starved to death by her stepfather in September 1985. Kimberly Carlile was starved, burned and battered to death by her stepfather in July 1986. Each of these cases was the subject of highly publicised inquests, trials and inquiries. Since the death of Maria Colwell, murdered by her stepfather in 1973, there have been 35 separate inquiries into the abuse of children in Britain. Horrific accounts of sex attacks on children and court cases featuring incest have become the standard fare of the tabloid press and the television news. The inquiry into the Cleveland child sex abuse controversy, involving the removal of 200 children from their families in the first half of 1987, focused the media spotlight on Middlesbrough town hall for five gruelling months.

The prolonged national outcry about child abuse has led to an ominous trend in official policy towards greater state intervention. The clamour over the ill-treatment of children has generated widespread fear and suspicion which has been exploited to full effect by the authorities. Judges, politicians and media pundits are united in demanding greater medical vigilance and more intensive surveillance by social workers of families identified as being at risk. Everybody agrees that the local authorities and the courts should be less reluctant to take repressive measures against families in which abuse is suspected.

Under successive governments the state has taken advantage of public concern about child abuse to extend its machinery of surveillance over society. In 1974, in response to the inquiry into the death of Maria Colwell, the department of health issued a circular entitled 'Non-accidental Injury to Children'. This proposed the formation of area review committees to monitor cases, periodic case conferences to coordinate all the agencies concerned with a particular family, and the establishment of registers of children deemed to be 'at risk'. Two years later the department produced an amended circular, recommending that the police should attend case conferences. A further circular in 1980 urged the formation of central register systems which covered not only physical ill-treatment, but also neglect and emotional abuse. Sexual abuse was added in 1986.

In December 1985 *A Child in Trust,* the report of the inquiry into the death of Jasmine Beckford, demanded a return to a more coercive role for social workers. In the fifties and sixties children had been commonly removed from what were designated as 'problem families' and raised in homes under the custody of the local authority. In the seventies policy swung away from institutional care in favour of keeping families together under the supervision of professionally trained social workers. Where natural parents could not look after their children, councils promoted fostering and adoption facilities rather than the old-fashioned children's homes. Social workers took on an essentially therapeutic role—'working with the family'—and the profession mushroomed. The 'care in the community' approach appealed to the authorities because it was cheaper than institutional care. It also corresponded with a widespread emphasis on 'parental rights' which united both right-wing and left-wing pressure groups. The aim of *A Child in Trust* was to swing the pendulum back in favour of a more interventionist role for state agencies dealing with families which fail to cope with the pressures of life in Thatcher's Britain.

Barrister Louis Blom-Cooper, chair of the Jasmine Beckford inquiry (and more recently of the Kimberly Carlile inquiry), insisted that the job of social workers should be to act as agents of social control when handling child abuse cases. ' "Authority" is not a dirty word,' stated the report, criticising social workers' reluctance to take on 'any authoritarian role in the enforcement of care orders'. The panel was adamant that social workers should enforce their legal powers to take children into care. The report concluded with a call for a more draconian approach to the protection of the child in trust: 'Society expects that a child at risk from abuse by its parents will be protected by social services personnel exercising parental powers effectively and authoritatively on behalf of society. Such a child is a child in trust.'

The Jasmine Beckford report also recommended a wider role for the police in dealing with child abuse cases. It insisted once again that the police should always attend case conferences on children at risk, and that they should be consulted before any care order was revoked or any child was taken off the 'at risk' register. Following these proposals another health department circular in May 1986 emphasised the need for close coordination among the different agencies. It acknowledged the importance of confidentiality, but insisted that 'ethical and statutory codes concerned with data protection are not intended to prevent the exchange of information between different professional staff with the objective of ensuring protection of children.' A professed concern for children's welfare allowed the authorities to build up a structure which can feed a vast amount of information about a particular family or local community straight into the police computer.

In July 1986 the government announced that local authorities, the health service, and independent schools would be granted access to criminal records to check any potential employee or volunteer working with children. Tory junior home office minister David Mellor claimed the impetus for this draconian decision came from the discovery that Colin Evans, who killed Marie Payne in December 1984, had been involved in voluntary work with children. In June 1987 more comprehensive vetting guidelines were issued to cover agency nurses, outside contractors and students training in nursing children. The government raised the possibility of extending the policing to voluntary organisations and private bodies providing services to children. The official announcement followed revelations that Surrey county council's education authority was already running a police check for criminal records on all its job applicants.

In July 1987 the home office announced that it was extending the maximum penalty for parents who wilfully neglect their children from a two-year to a 10-year prison sentence under a new clause in the Criminal Justice Bill. In January 1988 home secretary Douglas Hurd revealed that another new clause was to be added making it a criminal offence to possess child pornography. In the same month the education department disclosed that every state school would soon have a specially trained teacher able to spot abused pupils, under a scheme planned to start in spring 1988.

The official opening of the inquiry into the Cleveland controversy in August 1987 focused attention on the extensive use of the place-of-safety order: some 5500 are now issued every year. In law anybody can apply for such an order to detain a child under 17 and take him or her to a place of safety. The judge merely has to be satisfied that the applicant has reasonable cause to believe that the child is being abused or neglected. Most applications are made by professionals —doctors, social workers, teachers—who are under no legal obligation to inform the parents that it is planned.

At the end of 1987 the inquiries into the deaths of Kimberly Carlile and Tyra Henry finally ended with the publication of two reports. The report of the Kimberly Carlile inquiry, chaired by Louis Blom-Cooper, called for a severe clampdown on child abuse. *A Child in Mind* went several steps further than *A Child in Trust,* in recommending even tougher powers for police and social workers. But the central thrust of the report was the same: the call for a significant shift in emphasis from the claims of the parents towards the interests of the child.

Blom-Cooper's conclusion was that the child must be more firmly protected by the law:

'The principal duty of parents...is to make their child happy. If the parent fails in that regard, there can be no legitimate objection to the welfare authorities coming in to act for the child against the defaulting parent.'

The report demanded sweeping new powers for social workers, the police, the National Society for the Prevention of Cruelty to Children, GPs and health visitors. These range from the right to enter and see the child, a right to have the child medically examined, the right to apply for an emergency protection order to remove and detain the child, to the right of the police, social workers and NSPCC officers to enter and search without a warrant and inspect premises where a child thought to be at risk is living. 'Unfortunately the safety of a child sometimes has to infringe on civil liberties' declared Tory MP Geoffrey Dickens, who gave full backing to the proposals.

The establishment is following a perilous course in the child abuse controversy. How much farther can the state afford to encroach into the privacy and sanctuary of family life before it meets resistance? It has chosen to focus its moral crusade around an issue which if pushed is bound to lead to a questioning of established social norms.

It has used the panic about child abuse to introduce repressive powers into an arena where the consequences of an anti-state backlash could be devastating.

The perils of the child abuse panic have not escaped the notice of the more astute social commentators. The official message is that child abuse is an abomination, therefore the family must be cleaned up. The unofficial response could just as well be that child abuse is an abomination, so what does this tell us about family life under capitalism? The more the authorities insist on putting the blame on evil individuals and incompetent social workers, the more likely it is that people will start to reject the official scapegoats. Liberal *Guardian* columnist Melanie Phillips has seen through the Tories' attempts to stigmatise social workers:

> 'In crucifying them, we deflect attention from the real villains. A society which systematically starves, beats up, tortures, buggers and murders children is a deeply sick society. A society which does all these things and then sets up a group of Aunt Sallies to take the blame, turning the notion of doing good into the deepest insult, is even more vile.' (*Guardian*, 11 December 1987)

Phillips may have come to this conclusion because she has a soft spot for social workers, but the logic of her argument is faultless. While she concludes that we all share a collective guilt for the crime of child abuse, others might just as easily put the blame on the people responsible for running the system.

The difficulties for the establishment in making an issue out of child abuse without calling the family into question were experienced most acutely by the producers of Esther Rantzen's *ChildWatch* television show. The enormously successful programme went ahead only after it was given extra back-up from two social workers, an educational psychologist and the Broadcast Support Services workforce. Yet even this professional guidance could not resolve the problem the producers faced in trying to deal with child abuse without attacking the family. Executive producer Ritchie Cogan considered it essential that *ChildWatch* was seen as non-political and making no statements attacking the family: 'We had to be seen to be supporting the family, not attacking it' (*Independent*, 12 November 1986). Michele Elliott, a professional adviser for *ChildWatch*, added that it was as if 'we're saying the family is a sacred unit and children's rights come second.' Sean Cubitt from the Society for Education in Film and Television argued that *ChildWatch* was incapable of dealing with the fact that 'the family is as much part of the problem as the solution.' Even Esther Rantzen confessed that she tied herself in knots trying to deal effectively with child abuse and at the same time uphold the family.

The establishment's attempt to use force to achieve its own moral objectives in a sphere in which people resent outside interference more than in any other is another source of difficulties. The ruling class is on weak ground because its own traditional orthodoxy preaches the privacy and independence of the family, and, in the words of Ferdinand Mount, 'its rights to live according to its natural instincts'. Yet here is the state launching an unparalleled intrusion into the most private of family secrets. Writing in the *Financial Times,* John Lloyd pinpointed this dichotomy at the heart of the child abuse campaign:

'On the one hand, family values are seen as essentially private, providing sanctuary for child and adult alike, and the prevailing political culture tends to underpin this and frown on the intrusiveness of state or local agencies. On the other hand, powered by the graphic horror of the murders, the trend is towards more intervention and more intrusion.' (12 December 1987)

The child abuse problem places social workers in a predicament. If they follow the principle of 'leave well alone', they risk stern words from Blom-Cooper in the course of some future inquiry and worse at the hands of the gutter press. If they pursue the strategy of 'intervene at whatever cost', they risk the hostility of the invaded family. The real problem for the ruling class is that what started as a crusade to win public backing for a more repressive policing of morality, could well finish by unleashing a backlash against the authorities and ultimately the state. The potential for such a scenario has already been demonstrated by the popular reaction to the Cleveland and Tameside controversies.

The peculiar combination of a nationwide moral panic and a local team of paediatricians and social workers eager to put the principles of righteousness into practice resulted in the mass disruption of families in Cleveland. In May and June 1987 Dr Marietta Higgs and Dr Geoffrey Wyatt, together with the local social services department, were responsible for detaining children under place of safety orders at the rate of 25 a week. Parents who brought their children for routine out-patients' appointments or for casualty consultations found themselves subjected to summary court proceedings. The distress caused by the mass removal of children led to an angry backlash against the authorities. A local priest, the local MP and rival professional experts rallied to the side of the victimised families. A growing body of expert opinion was cautiously critical of the Cleveland paediatricians and social workers. Most of the children were subsequently returned to the care of their parents, many of whom have launched legal proceedings against the authorities.

In November 1987 anger exploded once again when Tameside council decided to make the unborn child of a local couple a ward of court at birth. The council announced that it intended to refuse access to Lily and Philip Rayner, whose baby was due in December, because three previous babies had died soon after birth. All three died in hospital from natural causes. The council's decision provoked a storm of protest by local people. Before the council had a chance to carry out its threat Lily Rayner went into premature labour and her baby was still-born. The Rayners have yet to receive a full account from the council of the motives for such draconian action.

Outraged by the council's action, local people handed in a 2000-signature petition of protest. Betty, a local lollipop lady who joined in the angry demonstrations, said that its actions could only reinforce suspicions against social workers. 'They're always picking on people. They say your house is dirty when it's not. They take your kids away from you, and it's always the likes of us that cop it.' Betty knows what she is talking about. When her baby died the police arrived the same day, put the baby in a bag, and 'carried it out like a bundle of washing'. Local fireman Bob said it was time to take a stand: 'Everyone here knows it's been an attack on working class people. The state's interfering in our lives. It's an insult to the Rayners, and it's an insult to the working class.' Months after the controversy, local people are still outraged.

Local people in Cleveland and Tameside showed a healthy distrust for the motives and the meddling of the authorities. Yet the establishment has been largely successful in spreading the panic among the general public. What should our attitude be to the child abuse issue, and how can we mobilise resistance to the mounting assault on our rights?

Never trust the state

Everybody is sickened by child abuse. But we should not allow our feelings of revulsion to blind us to the facts. We have yet to hear conclusive proof that there has been the explosion in child abuse that some authorities claim. Many polls claiming an incidence of child abuse that would be alarming if it were true have been discredited. In June 1987 the NSPCC announced a 137 per cent rise in child sexual abuse in 1986. The society reported that the increase was largely in abuse other than physical injury, such as emotional neglect and failure to thrive. NSPCC director Dr Alan Gilmour warned that it was impossible to say whether child abuse and neglect were increasing. What we can say is that higher public and professional awareness means that more cases are coming to light and being reported. Sexual abuse is notoriously difficult to define and thus to measure. Statistics are so heavily dependent on questions of definition and method as to be of no use in assessing a trend.

There can be no doubt that many children are physically and sexually abused. Around 100 children are murdered every year, many in their own homes, hundreds suffer appalling injuries, and thousands endure neglect and ill-treatment. Well-publicised cases of child abuse arouse widespread sympathy for the victims, anger against the perpetrators and frustration at the difficulties involved in tackling the problems. Yet agonising though the cases are, the problems are not new, and there is no good evidence that they are on the increase. So why is child abuse being given so much publicity now? Who benefits from the panic?

We have already seen that the state is the main beneficiary of a scare which has increased its powers to intervene in the lives of ordinary people. The NSPCC has undoubtedly benefited from the panic, and is now poised to take advantage of the impending Tory drive to break up local authority services and transfer responsibilities to voluntary organisations, charitable organisations and private provision. The papers, politicians and TV personalities have spread panic and indulged prurience for their own cynical purposes, whether it be to win readers, win public support for a moral crusade or boost viewing figures. The two categories of people who gain nothing from the child abuse panic are children at risk and the working class.

Just as having more policemen on the beat does not protect people in inner-city areas from crime, so more state surveillance and interference does not protect children from abuse. More police powers will not stop the deaths of more Jasmine Beckfords and Kimberly Carliles. Every public outcry in recent years has led to a new crop of referrals to social service departments and hospitals that cannot cope with their existing workloads. Encouraging children to report sexual abuse is of even more dubious value. Esther Rantzen's ChildLine appeal generated more phone-calls than could possibly be handled and left most unanswered. Even for those who were lucky enough to get through, there was no professional help available to sort out their problems. One inevitable consequence of the Cleveland fiasco is that parents will become so reluctant to bring their children to the local hospital that some may well suffer serious consequences from much more common illnesses like appendicitis or asthma.

The wider effect of the child abuse scare is to spread suspicion and distrust as everybody takes responsibility for policing their own friends and neighbours. This will have little impact on the most secret of family crimes and will protect few children from abuse. But it will help to keep everybody looking over their own shoulder. It will help to intensify the atomisation of individuals that is a characteristic feature of life in Thatcher's Britain. By encouraging a public preoccupation with private sexual deviations, it distracts people from wider political issues and strengthens the grip of the authorities over society.

One response to the problem of child abuse could be to encourage a different sort of community vigilance. Instead of the spying and informing on neighbours favoured by the establishment, working class people could take direct responsibility for the welfare of their own communities. By dealing with child abusers ourselves we could counter the corrosive influence of individualism in modern society, which isolates individuals in families and privatises social problems. We should *never,* however, invite state institutions to interfere in our communities on the pretext of dealing with child abuse.

The state appears in many different forms, from the riot policeman on a picket line to the friendlier face of those working in the welfare system. But however they are disguised as a force for good, and however sincere are the subjective motives of the individuals involved, state institutions exist solely to stabilise and defend the existing order.

As the servant of the capitalist class the state cannot solve our problems. Any reason it gives for involving itself more closely in our affairs is merely an excuse for tightening the grip of those who rule society. This goes for the 'soft' side of the state as well as its repressive machinery. For example, the social security system is a central component of the 'welfare state', which claims to ensure that the more vulnerable members of society are protected. Yet in reality it plays an important part in ensuring that millions live in poverty and misery, increasing the frustrations that people are likely to take out on each other—or on their children.

In the heat of the emotional arguments about child abuse many left wingers have lost sight of the issue of state interference. In the confusion surrounding the child abuse issue, the authorities are extending the powers of state agencies. Far from facing resistance, the government often finds radical opinion urging even more drastic state action. By strengthening the grip of reaction, this can only weaken the position of the working class. We must recognise that the state cannot play a useful role in protecting our children, and that the establishment is taking advantage of the child abuse scare to advance its own objectives. We should reject all attempts, however they are packaged, to increase state regulation of our lives. The working class must sort out its own problems, in the course of sorting out those who are responsible for our plight in the first place.

The family and freedom

Are we for or against the family? The question is misleading. The real issue is whether or not we go along with the establishment view of what the family should be. Let's summarise the argument so far.

The primary function of the family in modern society is to maintain and reproduce the working class. The family is the place where workers are reared and cared for from cradle to grave, and from generation to generation. This function is vital for a system founded on the exploitation of the working class. The economic arrangements that tie men and women to the family serve to restrict people's choices. Women bear the main responsibility for maintaining the fabric of family life, and are thus excluded from playing a full role in the life of society. The climate of recession has made people even more dependent on the family which compensates for declining welfare services and provides emotional solidarity.

The second function of the family is to police the working class. The family plays a key role in promoting respect for the established order, and in encouraging everybody to put their family commitments before their wider social responsibilities. This function is vital in a society based on the subordination of the majority of people to a minority which monopolises economic and political power. Family ideology brands alternatives to family life as immoral or illegal, especially at a time of social crisis. The Tories have launched a crusade to re-establish the family as a source of discipline and control, by bolstering parental authority and encouraging individuals to take responsibility for social problems. A key object of the Tories' elevation of family life is to strengthen individual preoccupations and undermine the possibility of collective action.

We are not against the family as such: for many people family relationships are a source of affection and intimacy. But we are opposed to the family as an instrument for perpetuating the exploitation of the working class, and the oppression of women, lesbians and gay men.

The working class has no interest in sustaining the family as an economic unit of the capitalist system. From this perspective the family has nothing to commend it to the working class in general or to women in particular. Capitalism offers no future to the working class and for women it means only continuing degradation. Our aim is to free the working class and women from exploitation and oppression, by overturning the system that has turned the family into a prison for so many people.

The liberation of women depends on making the work at present done by women in the family home—childcare, cooking, etc—part of the labour organised by society as a whole. The care of the family will become the concern of society instead of a burden on women. When the economic functions currently performed by the family are removed, then it will be possible for people to be free to make real choices about how and with whom they live.

The working class has no interest in allowing the authorities to use the family as an instrument of social control. Unlike the hypocrites who rule over society at our expense, we really are concerned about the damage that decaying capitalism does to working class lives. But we do not believe that we can resolve our problems by turning inwards to the family and trying to make the best of things on our own. Nor do we go along with the establishment's attempts to divert attention from our problems by scapegoating homosexuals and others. We believe that it is only by acting together as a class against the system which causes all these problems that we can achieve a society based on real social equality. Recognising that many people are attached to their families and to their personal lives, the ruling class seeks to manipulate these feelings to deter workers from fighting back. Yet it is only through united working class action that it is possible to rid society of the class of parasites that thrives on inequality and division.

3.
State regulation and social control

The state is assuming more and more powers to regulate sexual and moral behaviour. It does this through an expanding network of legislation, and through agencies such as social security and the social services which are becoming increasingly coercive. The prevailing orthodoxy holds that the state should intervene in the moral life of the nation only in exceptional circumstances. In reality such intervention is commonplace, and the capacity of the state to dictate how we live our lives is formidable. To understand the present tendency towards a more authoritarian supervision of sexuality and morality we need to look into its history.

The history of state interference in the sexual and moral sphere spans little more than a century. At particular moments the authorities have intervened decisively to assert control over the sexual practices and moral habits of its subjects. Such bursts of activity have generally been confined to periods of social change and crisis, which have given rise to movements demanding a return to traditional morality.

The first significant pieces of moral legislation were the Contagious Diseases Acts of 1864, 1866 and 1869. But these were an exceptional response to the specific problem of the spread of venereal infection in the armed forces. It was only from the 1880s onwards that the idea of state control over sexual and moral matters acquired wider acceptance. The growth of the social purity movement and the enactment of a series of repressive laws governing morality cannot be separated from the rise of popular nationalism and a preoccupation with the consequences of moral degeneration on the strength of British imperialism.

The Contagious Diseases Acts followed official investigations into the armed forces after the Crimean War. Inquiries revealed an alarming level of venereal disease and, in the opinion of the authorities, sexual immorality, among the lower ranks. The Contagious Diseases Acts sought to deal with venereal disease and the related social evil of prostitution. For the first time the medical profession was given full state backing in the sphere of public health. For 30 years medical and sanitary reformers had been campaigning to draw public attention to the link between cholera epidemics and the conditions of the working class. In the 1860s doctors and moralists succeeded in establishing the link between venereal disease and vice and won a position of power within the state.

The scope of the Contagious Diseases Acts was unprecedented. The 1864 Act applied to a number of naval ports and army garrison towns in England and Ireland. It gave police and doctors powers to notify a justice of the peace if they suspected a woman of being a 'common prostitute'. The woman would be taken to a certified hospital for medical examination, where she could be detained for up to three months. If she refused to comply she risked a two-month stretch in prison. The Acts of 1866 and 1869 extended the areas covered by the regulations, and mandated the Admiralty and the War Office to provide hospital facilities for inspection and treatment. The period of compulsory detention was extended to six months.

The medical profession, which had long been demanding state regulation of disease and immorality, enthusiastically supported the contagious diseases legislation. Doctors pushed for the extension of the Acts into a national system of inspection and detention of prostitutes and they were prominent in the Association for Promoting the Extension of the Contagious Diseases Acts to the Civilian Population. The medical profession celebrated the legislation as a symbol of its growing authority. But the real significance of the Acts was that they set a precedent of the state taking responsibility for the regulation of sexual conduct.

The Contagious Diseases Acts provoked opposition from a coalition of feminists, Liberals, Nonconformists and others, which succeeded in winning the repeal of the legislation in 1886. But many of the forces ranged against the Acts were later to come together in the social purity movement which campaigned for even more repressive laws in the sphere of sexual morality. Many opponents of the Contagious Diseases Acts did not object to state regulation in itself, but simply to the presumption of the legislation that women were the source of infection and hence were legitimate targets for repression. Many of the repeal campaigners were just as committed as the legislation's sponsors to the moral regeneration of the lower orders. But they blamed venereal disease and vice, not on female prostitutes, but on male depravity, arguing that the Acts penalised women unfairly while endorsing men's baser instincts. They believed that women, as the purer sex, had a major role to play in taming men's wild sexual urges. Once they had won the repeal of the offending Acts, it was quite consistent that the social purity campaigners should turn their energies to appealing to the state to outlaw immorality.

Social purity and the rise of nationalism

The first public opposition to the Acts came in October 1869 at a social science congress in Bristol. The newly founded National Anti-Contagious Diseases Acts Association excluded women from its first meeting, but later changed its policy. Meanwhile women led by Josephine Butler established the separatist Ladies' National Association. With the backing of prominent figures such as Florence Nightingale and Harriet Martineau, the association protested that the Acts were not only an attack on civil liberties but a symbol of state approval for male vice. The repeal campaign issued a two-fold challenge to the doctors. First, it disputed that the legislation had led to an improvement in morality, and issued voluminous statistics to prove it. Second, it argued that the law was incapable of changing moral behaviour, insisting that regeneration could only come about through educating people in self-control and personal morality.

Most repealers were supporters of the radical wing of the Liberal Party, and many were religious Nonconformists who were hostile to the established church and the corrupt establishment. The repeal campaign thus acquired a populist character, as its propagandists denounced the upper classes for their dissolute habits and double-standards. But in their moral convictions and anti-working class attitudes, the repealers had much in common with the upper classes whose decadence they despised. This was particularly apparent in the activities of the middle class movement.

The Ladies' National Association attacked the double-standard implicit in the Contagious Diseases Acts: 'The false idea that there is one code of morality for men and another for women...which has more or less coloured and shaped the whole of our social life' (Josephine Butler, 'Social Purity: An Address Given at Cambridge', 1879, cited in Mort, *Dangerous Sexualities,* 1987). For Butler and her supporters, male vice was the major cause of immorality. They argued that men who were incapable of controlling their lust, not women driven into prostitution, were responsible for moral corruption. Their conclusion was that virtuous women had a special role to play in reviving morality and saving the nation. This perception of women's missionary role in bringing about male redemption extended to the task of remoralising the working class. Many feminist reformers were involved in philanthropic work, especially in rehabilitating prostitutes. They were horrified by the licentiousness of the lower orders and intolerant of 'fallen women' who refused to repent their ways.

By the 1880s many former opponents of the Contagious Diseases Acts had overcome their aversion to state regulation. An alliance of clergymen, feminists and radical campaigners sought to persuade the Liberal government of William Gladstone to take punitive action against those who flouted the prevailing moral consensus. The National Vigilance Association, which numbered many feminists in its ranks, demanded the reform of male sexuality and coercive measures to enforce conformity. The social purity movement's emphasis on the need for legislation to deal with prostitution, homosexuality, indecency and obscenity signalled a decisive shift away from private philanthropy towards state control.

In the three decades before the First World War moralists and feminists came together in a campaign to increase the powers of the state over sexual and moral behaviour. According to one historian of the movement, social purity suffragettes 'wanted the state to act in its public health capacity as a moralising agency—to discourage promiscuity and encourage responsible sexual relations through moral education' (Lucy Bland, 'Cleansing the Portals of Life: The Venereal Disease Campaign in the Early Twentieth Century', in Mary Langan and Bill Schwartz (eds), *Crises in the British State, 1880-1920,* 1985). The purity feminists looked to the state to protect women and children, to educate men into self-control and chastity and to reform working class morals. The vigilance association argued forcefully against the old dogma that the law could not change public morality. The campaigners now insisted that the law could have an educative as well as a repressive function, acting as 'schoolmaster to the whole community'.

In the years from 1880 to 1920 the state massively extended its surveillance and regulation of morality. The 1885 Criminal Law Amendment Act, which criminalised all homosexual acts as gross indecency under the catch-all Labouchere clause, signalled the coercive trend. A spate of legislation followed, extending legal control over familiar areas such as indecency and prostitution, and creating new offences such as incest. New laws included the 1889 Indecent Advertisements Act, the 1898 Vagrancy Act (which criminalised male pimping and importuning) and the 1908 Incest Act. The 1912 Criminal Law Amendment Act increased penalties and police powers against procurers and brothel-keepers and clarified the scope of the 1898 Act to include male homosexuals. The 1922 Criminal Law Amendment Act abolished the 'reasonable cause to believe' clause in cases of indecent assault on girls under 16 and increased penalties for brothel-keeping. The 1929 Infant Life (Preservation) Act, which prohibited the killing of any child capable of being born alive, was the final achievement of the purity movement.

Mounting anxiety about the condition of the urban poor in the latter decades of the nineteenth century also provoked more state interference. Official government surveys such as the *Report of the Royal Commission on the Housing of the Working Classes* in 1884 revealed overcrowding, poverty, debauchery and incest on a scale that shocked the Victorian public. Middle class fears about the degeneracy of the 'unrespectable poor' were inflamed by the findings of other social investigators, journalists and novelists. The wretched condition of so many recruits for the Boer War (1899-1902) served to confirm the conclusions of Charles Booth, William Beveridge, Seebohm Rowntree and Hubert Llewellyn-Smith, who conducted pioneering surveys of urban life and poverty. Social investigators pointed to the existence of a degenerate underclass of the population, 'a residuum' which threatened the vitality of the nation. The revelations about the sorry state of the imperial army after the Boer War led to the fact-finding mission of the Inter-Departmental Committee on Physical Deterioration in 1904. The debate about national efficiency reflected ruling class anxieties about the future of the Empire at a time when it was being assailed by competition from abroad and growing unrest at home and in the colonies.

From the 1880s the state set about restoring the moral fibre of the

Empire. As early as 1880 the Industrial Schools Amendment Act proposed that courts should remove children from depraved and disorderly persons and place them in industrial schools. In the early 1900s the Liberal welfare reforms aimed to increase national efficiency and at the same time help to contain the growing labour unrest. The Labour Exchange Act, the National Insurance Act and the Development Act were sold to the employers, who had to pay a levy, on the grounds that they would profit from preventing the physical degeneration of the unemployed and from improvements in the morale of the working class that might deter enthusiasm for revolutionary socialism. Winston Churchill, a leading architect of the Liberal reforms, argued that there was 'no sentiment about it': the scheme would make the British worker 'a better citizen, a more efficient worker, a happier man' (cited in Jose Harris, *Unemployment and Politics,* 1972). A host of state institutions (ministry of health, labour exchanges, etc) and voluntary bodies (People's League of Health, Boy Scouts, etc) emerged, all committed to the improvement of the nation's health and morals.

Private morals and state controls: striking a balance

What pushed the state to step in as moral policeman? Today the left holds Tory backbencher Dame Jill Knight and her fellow bigots responsible for the success of Clause 28 of the Local Government Bill, which outlaws the 'positive promotion' of homosexuality. So too they claim that Liberal MP Henry Labouchere and his moralist supporters were responsible for the Labouchere clause outlawing all forms of male homosexuality. It is undoubtedly true that the social purity campaign became a highly effective pressure group, and a model for contemporary anti-abortion groups like Life and Spuc. But the idea that the impetus for legislation comes from the active lobbying of an autonomous movement which puts pressure on a disinterested state is misconceived. It derives from the commonplace radical view that the state is a neutral body standing above society, a view that has been reinforced by the promotion of morality as a universal ideology which transcends social class.

It is true that right up to the end of the nineteenth century the state was reluctant to intervene in moral matters. Even today the authorities exhibit caution in legislating about sexuality and morality. This is because the ruling class is keen to preserve the idea

God's cop James Anderton believes
that a moral code is more important
than a criminal law

that morality is God-given, and not the property of any particular class or party. In a recent article, top Tory adviser TE Utley pointed to the difficulties of using legislation as a direct means of 'making people good':

'Goodness, by definition, depends on a free exercise of will; the state, by definition, operates by applying public force to restrict the free exercise of will.' ('A Nation Sad to be Bad', *The Times,* 18 January 1988)

The message is clear: too much state coercion can only undermine the authorities' attempts to present morality as a universal virtue. Even a policeman like James Anderton recognises the advantages of keeping the law out of morality: 'I would argue that an acceptable moral code in this country is far more important than an enforceable criminal law' (Radio Four's *Sunday Programme,* January 1987). To keep up the pretence of impartiality, in parliamentary debates about divorce, homosexuality, the death penalty, suicide, abortion, etc, MPs are allowed to vote according to their consciences and party discipline is suspended.

The ruling class is aware that precipitate action runs the risk of provoking conflict over profound issues such as the role of the state, the function of the family, the oppression of women and homosexuals. When the National Birth Rate Commission reviewed sex hygiene teaching in 1920, minister of health Christopher Addison warned of the dangers:

'I think it is obvious that you touch subjects which are more nearly personal than any other class of topic, and in regard to which people as a whole resent, or are apt to resent, outside interference and direction more than any other.' (National Birth Rate Commission, *Youth and Race: The Development of Young Citizens for Worldly Parenthood,* 1923, cited in Mort, *Dangerous Sexualities*)

Recognising the problems involved in dictating a moral code, the establishment has always been careful to prepare the ground before issuing legally binding strictures. Thus TE Utley recently advised the establishment on how to proceed with its moral rearmament campaign: 'So long as the state does not run counter to prevailing moral convictions (which, we are told, are becoming increasingly conservative) it can do something, if it wishes, to promote the cause of traditional morality; but it must not be strident and it must be circumspect' (*The Times,* 18 January 1988). Thus the state has sought to strike a balance between the legal and the moral code, between formal legislation and informal controls enforced through state agencies and voluntary bodies.

The activities of the old social purity campaigners or modern-day moralists have never posed a problem for the state. Indeed such movements do sterling service for the establishment by preaching official morality among a wider audience. Their success has been due, not to the proficiency of their campaigning tactics, but to the fact that they have articulated the interests of the ruling class. In the late nineteenth century the social purity campaign flourished in the atmosphere of patriotic commitment and concern cultivated by the British capitalist class. Today's moralists thrive in the climate of Thatcherite reaction.

The ideas of the social purists and the increasing powers of the state did not go unchallenged. Some sections of the women's movement questioned the efficacy of using the state to protect women's interests. But their inability to challenge the morality that led many feminists to support state intervention rendered them incapable of mounting an effective challenge. The Women's Freedom League, for example, condemned punitive measures against prostitutes, yet argued feebly that the way forward lay in changing the moral outlook through economic and political reform.

Libertarian and utopian campaigners for sexual liberation also stood out against purity feminism. The Legitimation League, which was founded in 1893 and involved socialists such as Edward Carpenter, radical individualists like Orford Northcote and the American feminist Lillian Harman, argued for the liberalisation of the law and freedom in sexual relationships. But the individualistic approach of these sex reformers could not hope to challenge the all-class approach of the social purists. The most coherent opposition came from Sylvia Pankhurst's East End Suffrage Association, whose *Women's Dreadnought* pointed out that working class women were the victims of the state clampdown.

Unfortunately no movement emerged which was capable of directly taking on the social purity campaigners and the state offensive. Only a movement which mobilised opposition to the moralism and nationalism of the establishment by asserting the independent interests of the working class could have stood a chance of winning. That opportunity was thrown away in the period before the First World War by a socialist movement which never broke free from the grip of British chauvinism, and which never really confronted the issue of state oppression. So successful was the ruling class in building a consensus of support for a morality based on the family and the nation that it is only now, under the impact of the most profound social crisis of the post-war years, that we are once again in a position to take the initiative.

More than 2000 gay men are arrested every year for 'sex crimes' such as this

The creeping state

Britain in the late eighties is ripe for a re-run of the social purity movement. After the twenties there were no further additions to the criminal code on sexual and moral matters. When the state moved into this sphere once more in the fifties and sixties it was ostensibly to decriminalise many of the offences defined in the purity era—homosexuality, abortion, pornography. In reality the establishment was merely modifying the terms of state control in a period which saw a liberalisation of attitudes towards sex and morality. Economic expansion and unprecedented social harmony allowed for a relaxation of traditional taboos and a more permissive approach to sexuality. But the state never surrendered control, it simply re-established regulation on a new footing. Let's look more closely at the legislation of the 'permissive society' and how it is being reversed today.

●**Homosexuality**
The Sexual Offences Act of 1967 removed penalties against homosexual relations conducted in private between men over the age of 21. It maintained discrimination against homosexual men by stipulating a higher age of consent than for heterosexuals (21 rather than 16), and by imposing stringent conditions of privacy on homosexual relations. It amounted to a refinement of the criminal status of homosexual men, not the decriminalisation of homosexuality. The 1967 Act aimed to redraw the boundaries of what was considered acceptable sexual behaviour. It did not aim to liberate gay men (the law had never recognised lesbianism), but to proscribe public displays of homosexuality by tolerating it 'between consenting adults in private'. In a speech supporting the Act in the upper house, Lord Arran captured the spirit in which it was passed: 'I ask those who have, as it were, been in bondage and for whom the prison doors are now open to show their thanks by comporting themselves quietly and with dignity.' Gays were still regarded as perverts, but so long as they kept their deviancy to themselves society would tolerate them.

Clause 28 of the Local Government Bill signals the end of the more liberal attitudes towards homosexuality. It is the most far-reaching legal attack on the rights of homosexual people since the Labouchere amendment in 1885 and the Vagrancy Act of 1898. Margaret Thatcher's government has given the go-ahead to Clause 28 as part of an effort to crush the gay scene and to drive homosexuals out of public life. It will lead to a more rigorous use of the Sexual Offences Act alongside raids, arrests and witch-hunts. Clause 28 makes 'queer-bashing' official state policy. Breaking with the long-established tradition of free voting on so-called 'issues of conscience', the government imposed a three-line whip to ensure a safe passage for the clause.

There is now no middle ground when it comes to the issue of homosexual rights. The choice is between promoting a pogrom against lesbians and gays and fighting for the decriminalisation of homosexuality. Our slogan must be *Equal Rights for All, Fight for Lesbian and Gay Rights.*

●Abortion

The 1967 Abortion Act allowed abortion only under certain circumstances. The 'green form' specifies that abortion is permissible when a woman can satisfy two doctors that the pregnancy puts her own life in danger, threatens the welfare of her existing children, or that there is a substantial risk of the baby being born seriously handicapped. An additional clause allows abortion on the grounds that 'the continuation of the pregnancy would involve a risk of injury to the physical or mental health of the pregnant woman greater than if the pregnancy were terminated'. This is the tenuous basis on which the vast majority of women gain permission from doctors and the state to have an unwanted pregnancy terminated. The Act did not eliminate the offence of child destruction outlawed by earlier legislation, and the viability limit of 28 weeks remained in force.

The 1967 Act did not legalise abortion: it remained illegal except under stringent conditions. There was no liberating impulse behind the 1967 Abortion Act: it gave new rights to doctors, not to women. The new legislation was motivated by the need for the state to step in to regulate practices which were already widespread. It aimed to remove abortion from the backstreets and bring it firmly official/medical control.

Liberal MP David Alton's attempt to impose further restrictions on women seeking abortions, by reducing the legal time-limit for terminations to 18 weeks, signals the start of a concerted attack on abortion rights. A rearguard action began almost as soon as the 1967 Act became law, and there have been more than a dozen attempts to amend the law. But it is only now, in Thatcher's third term, that the anti-abortion lobby looks like succeeding. The moralists have worked hard to turn public opinion against providing access to abortion. They have been helped along by strident anti-abortion groups such as the Society for the Protection of the Unborn Child and Life. The combination of anti-abortion propaganda and cuts in resources and facilities has pushed half the women who need abortions into the private sector.

Every woman should have the right to abortion without seeking permission from doctors and without legislative restriction. Our slogan must be *Free Abortion on Demand–As Early as Possible, As Late as Necessary.*

● **Censorship**

The relaxation of censorship was in many ways the most conspicuous feature of the permissive society. The sixties opened with the sensational failure of the prosecution against Penguin Books under the 1959 Obscene Publications Act for publishing DH Lawrence's novel *Lady Chatterley's Lover.* 'Would you allow your wife or servant to read this book?' the prosecuting counsel asked the jury. The presumed reply of the jury in delivering the 'not guilty' verdict set the tone for the decade. Throughout the sixties the state was reluctant to use the Obscene Publications Act to restrict publishing, and attempts to impose censorship through legal action generally failed. Even when prosecutions were successful, as in the case of the novel *Last Exit to Brooklyn,* the authorities made no effort to enforce the ruling and prevent the distribution of the book. The temporary retreat from state censorship was summed up in the abolition in 1968 of the power of the Lord Chamberlain to censor theatrical productions. The media featured sex more explicitly than before. The *Sun* first appeared in 1964 and soon made 'page 3' synonymous with pictures of naked women. 'Four letter words' were heard in television dramas and 'full frontal' nudity became acceptable on television and at the cinema. The relaxation of censorship allowed the pornography industry to flourish, bringing a wide range of sexually explicit glossy magazines into most high street newsagents.

The recent formation of a home office committee to regulate sex and violence on television is only the latest example of the return of the censors. The clamour for censorship began almost as soon as the sixties were over, when Mary Whitehouse launched the National Viewers and Listeners Association in 1971. In 1976 James Anderton took over as Manchester police chief and launched a crusade against pornography and prostitution. His special squads raided 264 bookshops, newsagents and warehouses in his first year, even seizing copies of the *Sun's Page 3 Girl* annual. Asked by the *Guardian* whether his excessive zeal might not conflict with individual freedom, Anderton gave a characteristically censorious and eccentric reply: 'Freedom to do what? To have sexual intercourse on the pavement in front of our house? What do you want me to do? Show them films of bestiality?' (Cited in the *Guardian,* 21 January 1987).

In 1984 customs officials swooped on London's Gay's the Word bookshop and confiscated large numbers of books. Graham Bright's bill to impose censorship on video recordings became law after a year of hysterical reports about the corrupting effect of 'video nasties' on the nation's children. In 1987 Tory MP Winston Churchill's bill to extend the Obscene Publications Act to cover audible and visual publications failed to become law, but received wide support from all parties. In 1987 Whitehouse denounced Dennis Potter's award-winning television play *The Singing Detective* for 'gross sexual violence', the smut-sheet daily *Star* promised to be more restrained, Radio One banned George Michael's single 'I Want Your Sex' until after 9pm and the IBA apologised for showing Joan Collins' *Sins* during prime-time family viewing. Next they'll be banning left-wing newspapers and censoring political films.

As the clamour for censorship gets louder our response is to reject all restrictions on the media. Our demand must be *No to the Official Morality, No Bans on Our Rights.*

The trend towards moral authoritarianism threatens further infringements of our rights—even under existing legislation. The law on sexual offences covers rape, 10 'other offences involving sexual intercourse', three categories of indecent assault and indecency with children, six offences relating to the abduction of women, five offences relating to prostitution, two offences of indecent exposure, and finally six 'unnatural offences'. The law on public morals covers a host of bigamy offences, two further offences relating to marriage, about a dozen obscenity offences, and of course blasphemy. There is enormous scope to bring moral charges under public order or state security legislation. Laws covering abortion or infanticide may be extended to restrict termination of pregnancy, *in-vitro* fertilisation and embryo research.

In the sphere of informal control too the trend is towards more proscriptive measures against offenders of society's moral code. Let's look at a few examples.

●The welfare state

'A friend of mine used to come down and stay at the weekends—I used to put him up on the sofa. Early one Monday morning a man from the social security paid an "unannounced visit". It turned out they'd been watching the flat and had seen Steve leave one morning. When this investigator came in he asked if he could use the loo, but he only went in to snoop and he found Steve's shaving cream. He said we were cohabiting and Steve would have to support me. If you'd seen him you'd see why I wasn't cohabiting with him. But the social security said I was and threatened to take me to court.' (Cited in *the next step,* 9 May 1986)

Sue, an unemployed single woman, had just had a visit from a social security sex snooper. The cohabitation rule allows social security staff to interrogate claimants about the most intimate aspects of their lives. It allows them to poke around bedrooms and bathrooms, looking for evidence of sexual activity. Thousands of women lose their benefits every year because of this. Yet the rule works much more widely by making women feel afraid and ashamed of claiming benefits. It deters many women from claiming, forcing them to rely on men, and keeps others in a constant state of guilt and fear about having sexual relationships while they are on the dole. Either way the state saves money and encourages its favoured family values.

The welfare authorities have further coercive powers. Under the terms of the new Tory Employment Bill unemployed people under the age of 18 will be denied benefit unless they accept a two-year YTS placement. Again, the state saves money, and restricts the options of young people. Youth training conscription is only the latest move by the welfare state to keep unemployed youth off the streets and out of trouble.

●**The education system**
'Just as schools have a role in passing on moral values, so they must promote the fundamental political values that sustain our society' declared Tory education minister Chris Patten in 1986, in a candid admission about the true function of the British education system. His forthright statement was in keeping with the higher profile role of the schools in maintaining social discipline. It seems that the main function of schools now is to train their pupils to be responsible parents and patriotic citizens. Sex education classes have become particularly important in promoting conventional family values. Hence in 1986 the Tories amended the Education Act to include a stipulation that sex education must be presented to pupils 'in such a way as to encourage those pupils to have due regard to moral considerations and the value of family life'. The Love and Marriage amendment, as it became known, was just another attempt to impose capitalist discipline, respect for authority and contempt for

women's rights on the next generation of the working class.

When the Tories want to use schools for propaganda purposes this is depicted as being in the best interests of the nation's children. On the other hand, any trace of anti-establishment ideas in schools is denounced as political indoctrination and a threat to the British way of life. Subjects such as sociology and peace studies and discussions about racism or imperialism are condemned as a cause of declining standards. Teachers who supposedly drum homosexuality into young children, by making them read books such as (the unobtainable) *Jenny Lives with Eric and Martin,* will be dealt with by new government legislation. The government plans to allow schools to become independent of the local education authority, to turn headmasters into managers with full financial control, to introduce a national core curriculum and to increase subsidies to public schools. All these measures threaten to make the education system even more alienating for working class children.

●The social services

'This case involves two children whose parents separated, a girl and a boy aged 13 and 12. When I started visiting, I felt the father was looking after them fairly well. But then, after about a year, things began to slide. The father was out of work and ran into financial difficulties. The children were made wards of court and we were given leave to find foster homes. Unfortunately, the children had learned to be quite manipulative, and spent a good deal of the time running away. Eventually, the foster mother couldn't cope and they went to a children's home. We were able to help the father financially and with improvements in the home. The children are back with the father now and they seem much more settled.' (Cited in the *Listener,* 6 February 1986)

A Hackney social worker details an unexceptional case which in her view had a 'happy ending'. It provides some insight into the role of social workers in policing the lives of millions of ordinary people. Social work is an official mystery. Nobody seems to know how many there are, although some suggest around 25 000 are employed by local authorities and thousands more work for voluntary agencies. Local authorities are required by law to hire adequate staff and appoint a director for their social services activities. In reality few if any local authorities have sufficient staff or resources to cope with the elderly, the homeless, the impoverished, the mentally ill, the sick and infirm, the battered children, the single parents and the countless others in need of help.

Social workers counsel people on their personal problems and enforce official solutions. The recent drift towards tougher intervention and more coordination with police and other agencies means more rigorous supervision over the lives of working class people. As the climate of hysteria over child abuse has intensified, social workers have often been pilloried by the press and sometimes physically assaulted by members of the public. But that is the price they pay for playing the role of soft policemen for a ruling class which regards repression as the solution for every social problem. The real losers are not social workers, but the people on the receiving end of a degrading and violent system.

We should not forget the services rendered to the state by the Manpower Services Commission, the British Medical Association, the churches, youth organisations and countless voluntary bodies which all play a part in policing morality. The soft arm of the state might be less coercive than its repressive apparatus, but it shares the same objectives. We should be just as vigilant in resisting the encroachment of these institutions on our rights, as we are in challenging the creeping authoritarianism of the strong-arm state.

Just say no

Resistance to the state has been dogged by the widespread belief that the state is a neutral body which can be persuaded to defend the interests of all. This faith in the state's powers to do good has led women's rights campaigners and left-wing groups to demand tougher laws against pornography and rape to protect women from sexual abuse. Some feminists and radicals have opposed these demands on the grounds that they invite state repression and do nothing to defend women. But confusion about the issues involved and about the role of the state has blocked the emergence of a movement committed to fighting for women's rights independently of the state machine. Public debates on pornography and rape have strengthened the moral standards and state institutions that maintain women's oppression.

Pornography has been condemned from across the political spectrum, from far-right Manchester police chief James Anderton to left-wing Labour MP Clare Short. Anderton recently spoke out against public nudity:

'It offends me to see topless pictures because it cheapens the image of women. Sex is not there to cause temporary excitement. It shouldn't be paraded for people to talk about, laugh at and, worse still, titillate the sexual emotions of the opposite sex. It's highly debatable whether or not a page 3 photograph of a young woman will excite someone to commit a sexual offence, but it's the starting point. It is not harmless fun.' (*Woman's Own*, 19 December 1987)

On all this Clare Short would heartily agree. In 1986 she introduced a 10-minute bill calling for a ban on newspaper nudes on the grounds that they lead to rape and other violence against women. This was proposed as an amendment to Winston Churchill's bill to restrict the representation of obscene, violent or sexual material on TV, which she fully supported along with most other Labour MPs. Now Clare Short and fellow MP Jo Richardson are preparing another bill, with the backing of the National Council for Civil Liberties, to outlaw 'sex discrimination through pornography'. Their views are endorsed by feminists like Andrea Dworkin who argue that pornography causes men to see women as sex objects, and leads inevitably to rape.

While pornography is undoubtedly degrading to women, we cannot support either Anderton or Short in demanding more state censorship. Pornography is not the cause of women's oppression, and banning it will do nothing to rescue women from their second class status in society. The depiction of women as sex objects is merely a reflection of our inferior position in the real world. Doing away with pornography will not alter the social relations of capitalist society which are the cause of our oppression. Nor would it prevent rape: rape was just as common in Victorian times when women's bodies were hidden from view, and during the fifties when strict censorship prevailed. Degradation, violence and rape can only be fought by freeing women from domestic drudgery and isolation, and from economic dependence. Dworkin is right that 'women will know they are free when pornography no longer exists' (Andrea Dworkin, *Pornography: Men Possessing Women,* 1979). But freedom for women will not come about by passing a parliamentary bill to ban page 3, but through a struggle to overturn a system built on oppression.

The real question raised by the pornography debate is whether we are for or against state censorship. If Short succeeded in getting rid of page 3 it might undermine the *Sun's* position in the tabloid circulation war. But it would strengthen the state's hand in imposing more extensive censorship. More censorship would particularly affect lesbians and gay men, whose sexuality is already considered obscene by the authorities. Homosexuals living in Manchester have frequently suffered the consequences of James Anderton's aversion to 'pornography', at the hands of his special squads which raid their bookshops and nightclubs and hunt down gays in public lavatories. Brian Derbyshire, editor of *National Gay* newspaper, rightly argues that censorship of pornography leads to the promotion of women's place in the family and a crackdown on homosexuality:

'At the moment the politicians are all screaming about the virtues of the family. This gives the police carte blanche to do anything they want. Censorship would only make the police stronger and us weaker because they'd use it to harass women and gays.'

The clamour for censorship has already led the Inner London Education Authority to withdraw *Jenny Lives with Eric and Martin*, and to doctor a resources guide for teaching about homosexuality. It was also obliged to scrap the flyer to its *Anti-sexist Resources Guide* because it mentioned the Belfast Women's Centre which Ilea feared the press might expose as pro-IRA bias. It has also withdrawn its *Auschwitz* teaching pack dealing with the Nazi holocaust and racism, and its teaching pack on contraception. Calls for more censorship can only give the state greater authority to define what is obscene—today it is *Capital Gay*, tomorrow it could be this book.

The Tories have steadily increased their pressure on the media to conform with the Thatcher worldview. Norman Tebbit carpeted Kate Adie and the BBC for her reports on the joint US-British air-raid against Libya. The government has gone to extraordinary lengths to suppress information about 'state security' issues, hounding former MI5 spycatcher Peter Wright and the intrepid *New Statesman* whistleblower Duncan Campbell with equal venom. British troops have tried to disrupt the distribution of Sinn Fein's weekly newspaper *An Phoblacht/Republican News*. Next they will be banning left-wing papers and radical films. We can agree with the English Collective of Prostitutes which opposes censorship 'because basically we do not think the state or any other body should have the power to decide what the individual should do or see' (cited in Terence Du Quesne & Edward Goodman, *Britain: An Unfree Country*, 1986). But we go further. We are opposed to censorship because we are not prepared to aid our enemies by helping them to impose their own standards of morality on the working class, and because our objective is to dismantle the state machine not add to its repressive apparatus.

Rape is another issue which has led to unlikely alliances between right-wing fanatics and left-wing radicals. From far-right Tories like Geoffrey Dickens to Labour left stalwarts like Dennis Skinner, politicians are united in calling for tougher sentences for rapists. The outcry over the sentencing of the Ealing Vicarage rapists in February 1987 was typical of the way in which women's groups and the left are now lining up behind the authorities in demanding more law and order measures to deal with rapists. Despite the particularly brutal character of the rape, Mr Justice Leonard sentenced the two rapists to three and five years' imprisonment, saying 'The trauma suffered by the victim was not so great.' He jailed a third man, not involved in the rape but accused of aggravated burglary, for 14 years.

The press, the police, politicians—even the saintly Ealing vicar—all condemned the judge for punishing theft more heavily than rape. They emphasised their concern to deter rape by punishing rapists harshly. The universal call for heavier policing and tougher sentencing was echoed by many women's groups and left wingers. But we should be suspicious of establishment figures whose past record shows a singular lack of concern about women's welfare, and who profess a sudden concern to do something about it when rape hits the headlines.

Rape is the most extreme manifestation of women's oppression in modern society. But rape is far from the only way in which women are brutalised. Violence against women is endemic in a system which degrades women in the home and at work. In a system which treats women as second class citizens it is scarcely surprising that men feel free to abuse them. Contrary to the media myth, rape is not generally the act of a psychopathic sex maniac. More women are raped at home than in any other place and most rapists are known to the victim. They are husbands and boyfriends, friends and relatives, neighbours and workmates.

The same politicians who preach concern about rape are supporters of the status quo that keeps women at the bottom in the home and at work. The police who have pledged to do more to combat rape are well-known for turning a blind eye when women report beatings by their husbands. Thousands of women have found them anything but protective when it comes to rape. A survey by Women Against Rape revealed that 90 per cent of women who are raped refuse to report it to the police for fear of interrogation, abuse and humiliation. Many women have found their experience in the police station as degrading as the rape itself.

The judges who preside over rape cases are notorious bigots and misogynists. In January 1988 Darlington magistrate Charles Garraway told a man who head-butted and punched his girlfriend that 'we don't expect a boyfriend to punch his girlfriend...slap her once or twice but don't punch her' (*Independent,* 8 January 1988). Rapists are often excused on the grounds that they were 'led on'. In October 1987 deputy high court judge Sir Frederick Lawson declared that a 14-year old rape victim 'seems to me to be a menace to young men' (cited in *the next step,* 6 November 1987). In January 1988 Mr Justice Owen from Lincoln said that he considered the rape of a 12-year old virgin to be at 'the lower end of rape'. He added that 'in other days one would have said she was asking for trouble' in a clumsy attempt to impute that *he* was not saying so *now* (*Daily Mirror,* 13 January 1988). The press pilloried the judge who passed the paltry sentence in the Ealing case, but went to great lengths to give the gruesome details of the rape to titillate their readers. Why should we put our faith in press, police and politicians who preach prejudice against women 51 weeks of the year and in the other one make a fuss about sex crimes because it suits their purpose?

The effect of the media preoccupation with rape is to direct people's revulsion into a crusade to strengthen the authority of the police and the courts. Rape is a good issue around which to rally support for more law and order because everybody feels sorry for the victims and angry about the assailants. But, as the Women Against Rape survey notes, 'Long sentences are often advocated for reasons which have nothing to do with women's safety.' The establishment manipulates public outrage about rape to create a climate favourable to more repressive laws. The beneficiaries of extra police and legal powers are not women, but the system that brutalises them.

Putting more police on the streets and sanctioning stronger sentences will not stop women being raped. In fact more regimentation of life can only make matters worse for women. Whatever new weapons the police and the men in wigs are given, they will use them to defend the powers of those who rule over us. The system's legal guardians will always put protecting private property first, as they did in Ealing. After all the rape case controversies, a clause in the Criminal Justice Bill to give appeal court judges the power to recommend increased sentences is now expected to sail through parliament. Who benefits? Only the ruling class.

The debates around rape and pornography show the dangers of demanding state responses that can only strengthen the forces of the establishment. Ultimately all state powers will be used against the oppressed and exploited to defend the privileges of the ruling class. As much as we would like to get rid of pornography and get even with rapists we cannot afford to let our anger be channelled into a campaign for more censorship or more repression. The only effective way to take a stand against pornography and rape is to fight for women's rights against the system that degrades us all. We will not succeed by putting more powers in the hands of our oppressors.

**The famous thumb-sucking,
body-popping fetus**

4.
Abortion and women's rights

Y ou have probably seen him. He is 18 weeks old and sucking his
thumb. His picture has been featured in most of the national dailies.
He has been mounted on one million postcards and despatched to
parliament. In 10 weeks' time he will be able to dance to pop music,
he will have taken a shine to brass bands, developed an aversion to
smokers, and acquired a sweet tooth. These are only a few
astonishing facts about 'the secret life of a fetus' as featured in the
tabloid press. You probably know the rest. This particular fetus,
whose picture dates back 20 years, has become the symbol of the pro-
life lobby in its campaign to amend the abortion law.

You may have been following the unfolding story of Michelle's
pregnancy in *EastEnders*, either on television or in conversations
with any of the six million regular watchers. Norman Tebbit has
certainly seen it and is not impressed. Many thousands of women
who saw the episode in which Michelle pleaded her case before an
abortion counsellor could not have failed to be struck by the

familiarity of the situation. Michelle's convincing portrayal of the suffering experienced by a woman having to cope with an unwanted pregnancy was a powerful rejoinder to the anti-abortionists. The response of her family and friends to Michelle's pregnancy was all too typical of the way in which women are pressurised into going ahead and having babies they do not want.

These are two popular presentations of the opposing sides in the abortion debate. Scarcely a day goes by without the media adding some new angle to the discussion. There has been a seemingly endless series of demonstrations and counter-demonstrations by opponents and supporters of abortion rights. Let's look first at the arguments of the pro-life lobby.

Moral absolutes against abortion

The view that a fetus is a potential human being which has the same right to life as any person is widely held even by people who are not strongly religious. This is the most profound argument against women's right to abortion, and it is the central theme of the supporters of the Alton Bill. Tory MP Ann Widdecombe, a keen campaigner for the Society for the Protection of the Unborn Child and for Life, is adamant that the key issue is the sanctity of fetal life:

'The 1967 Abortion Act was a piece of moral and legislative hypocrisy ignoring the central issue, which was, and still is, the definition of life itself. Is the unborn child a human being? If the answer to that question is "Yes", then clearly that child should enjoy normal human rights, the most fundamental of which is the right to life itself. If the answer is "No", then there should be no need for legislation to protect the fetus.' (Cited in *News on Sunday*, 25 October 1987)

Anti-abortionists like Widdecombe are eager to draw out the contradiction in a piece of legislation that denies the absolute right to life of the fetus, and at the same time denies the absolute right of women to abortion. For the pro-life lobby there is no middle ground.

The absolute moral principle of the sanctity of life is constantly proclaimed by today's moral campaigners. Journalist Ronald Butt, a leading philosopher of the new right, insists that principle must come before pragmatism:

'If it is hard to make a moral distinction between the abortion of a viable child and infanticide, it must follow that it isn't easy to make a distinction between the abortion of a viable child and an earlier one to prevent the fetus reaching the threshold of viability. It is still the destruction of human life.' ('Abortion Bare of Illusion', *The Times*, 26 February 1987)

84

Some anti-abortionists have argued that the left would support the right to life if it was really concerned with the future of humanity. Charles Moore, editor of the *Spectator,* argues that the left's concern to assert the dignity of man in the face of military aggression and ruthless competitiveness should be extended to embrace the inalienable rights of the fetus. The new moralists thus proclaim a universal right to life.

It follows that women have no rights over and above the fetus. Taking his argument one step further, Moore states that the moral code cannot sanction abortion on any grounds:

'The choice of abortion assures rights over a new life by the woman who happens to be the custodian of that life for nine months. Where do those rights come from? Unless this question can be answered the choice of abortion cannot be made. People are now beginning to notice that no good answer to the question has been forthcoming.' ('A Signpost towards a Moral Society', *Daily Telegraph,* 22 October 1987)

The traditionalists particularly object to those who argue that although abortion is not positively desirable, there is nothing wrong with it if a woman has conceived an unwanted child. They denounce those who have devalued human life by turning abortion into a convenience. Consultant gynaecologist Pamela Simms gave full backing to this prejudice with her statement that 'we are talking about women who don't want a child because it spoils next year's holiday, or because they would rather have a boat instead' (*Independent,* 28 October 1987).

How do the moralists explain what they regard as the mass depravity of those who have abortions? This is the question to which they return again and again; and the answer is always the same—the evil permissive society of the sixties. Speaking at a Life rally in support of the Alton Bill last October, Tory MP Alistair Burt argued that the aim of the campaign was not simply to outlaw abortion, but to re-establish moral absolutism:

'The sixties were a time of great selfishness, compounded by the seventies "me" generation. Improvements in the standard of living have meant that many people lack for nothing except a soul. We will turn away from the Godlessness of the sixties. It is not a return to old values or new ones, but to moral values which are absolute.' (27 October 1987)

The conviction that the selfishness and consumerism of the sixties and seventies have sponsored a casual disregard for values once held to be eternal is common to the new right. Paul Johnson, writing in the *Spectator,* decried the way in which the child in the womb has become 'disposable'—'like panty-hose or plastic cartons' (5 December 1987).

Butt takes a more reflective view of the degeneration brought about by permissiveness:

'The old restraints that once governed conduct have been dismantled and new conventions created, which begin with the way in which children are taught about sex. Chastity is not to be taught because that is moralising; contraception is better than abortion, but in the end abortion is far better than an unwanted child. It has been morally respectable, if regrettable, for life to be conceived only to be destroyed within 28 weeks.' (*The Times,* 26 February 1987)

Butt's not so original thesis is that once the old moral taboos are abandoned perversions will flourish and society will degenerate.

The anti-permissive moralists never tire of tracing the inner connections among the social evils that make up the sum of the contemporary malaise. Writing in the *Daily Telegraph,* Charles Moore recently noted how one thing inevitably led to another:

'The question of abortion cannot be isolated from the social and moral changes of the past 20 or more years. People increasingly complain of a lack of respect for our common humanity. This is manifested in numerous ways. It is visible in crime, particularly violent crime, and in vandalism; it is visible in more minor matters like rudeness or impatience. It is apparent in commercial greed and in the commercial exploitation of sex. It is vividly present in children's loss of innocence and in their sexual abuse.' (22 October 1987)

Here we have the familiar litany of complaints about the crimes of permissiveness and its contemporary victims. For Pamela Simms too, abortion is the prime source of moral evil. 'Is the abortion mentality part of what is wrong with our society today? Is it mere coincidence that the value of human life seems to have been cheapened—that alongside abortion we have escalating child abuse, muggings of the elderly and so on?' (*Independent,* 29 October 1987). The message is that what was originally presented as something which would benefit women and humanity as a whole has proved to be a disaster. This was the theme of an editorial in the *Spectator,* which argued that the feminism and liberalism of the sixties had led up a moral cul-de-sac:

'There has never been a time when people have known as much as they do now about sex. There has also never been a time of so much child abuse, illegitimacy, abortion and divorce. Is it not possible that the breaking down of taboo has also broken down a moral tradition which enabled people, though poor, to cherish new life? A society which offers abortion or childbirth as almost equally acceptable alternatives does not do away with the sad phenomenon of an unwanted child. It makes children more likely to be unwanted. It encourages picking and choosing,

Neither David Steel (above), who
created the 1967 Abortion Act, nor
David Alton
(left), who seeks
to amend it,
give any
credence to the
issue of
women's rights

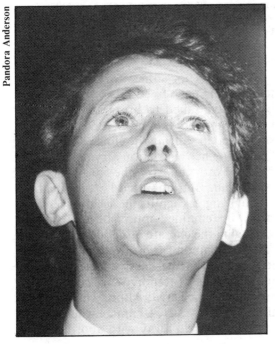

throwing away those who might, for example, be disabled, as a stallholder might throw away bruised fruit. It allows the value of a future life to be assessed according to other people's criteria, and gives no independent right to that life at all.' (24 October 1987)

The anti-abortionists insist that the spread of sex education, freely available contraception and the liberalising of abortion have not brought any reduction in sexual or marital problems. They cite the rising levels of divorce, illegitimacy and child abuse as proof that permissiveness has not worked. Their contention is that 'a woman's right to choose' has not produced the right choices, nor much happiness.

The moralists' most sophisticated argument is that women are the real victims of permissiveness. Many anti-abortionists put themselves forward as the true defenders of women's interests. They contend that abortion is an instrument of male power. From the point of view of men, abortion is convenient and painless. For women it entails distress and suffering. At the heart of the argument, however, is the view that abortion is a violation of motherhood:

'It means having to refuse the creative role unique to the female sex. Surely, then, abortion is an attack on what it is to be a woman. Surely feminists should see that it is an attack which comes mainly from men?' (*Spectator,* 24 October 1987)

Pro-lifers can produce surveys and statistics to prove, at least to their own satisfaction, that abortion is traumatic for the vast majority of women. They remind their opponents that the recipients of three million abortions since 1967 have not come forward in their thousands to extol and defend their new 'freedom'.

So far the anti-abortionists have failed to bring about a single alteration to the existing law (see appendix for a full account of their attempts). But they have succeeded in shifting the climate of opinion towards an acceptance of some further restriction on women's right to abortion. In fact many exponents of the pro-life cause acknowledge that this is their aim. Butt admitted he was sceptical about the prospects for achieving a significant legal reverse to women's right to abortion. But he remained optimistic nevertheless: 'I am not sceptical about changing the climate of opinion. There are clear signs of changing attitudes among more thoughtful young people about abortion and the rest of the permissive society's legacy, and they will be the opinion-formers of tomorrow' (*The Times,* 26 February 1987). This too is the aim of David Alton, who concedes that the purpose of his initiative is to 'create a climate where people don't want abortions', rather than to do away with abortion now:

'Legislation is a way of changing the climate of the times' (cited in *New Statesman,* 15 January 1988).

How has the anti-abortion lobby gone about changing 'the climate of the times'? It has become adept at creating controversy around particular cases and manipulating the media to publicise its cause. In a case last year the courts jailed Trevor Virgo from London under the Infant Life (Preservation) Act, after he was convicted of a vicious attack on his pregnant ex-girlfriend Julie Wolton. Virgo stripped her in the snow, then kicked and punched her until she had a miscarriage. Virgo got 16 years for assaulting Wolton, but life for destroying the unborn baby. Wolton was 28 weeks' pregnant, the legal cut-off point after which a fetus is deemed 'capable of being born alive'. The media concentrated its coverage on the destruction of the fetus, and all but ignored the woman's own injuries. 'Monster gets life for kicking his unborn baby to death' screamed the *Sun's* front page. It was only the seventh time that the 1929 Act had been used in recent history. The significance of the case lay in the fact that it took place amid mounting coverage of the abortion issue. The idea that an unborn baby can be 'murdered', and that its fate is more important than the health of the woman carrying it, gives legal sanction to the 'embryo rights' lobby, which has used such arguments to attack women's rights to abortion.

Another notable landmark in the crusade against abortion was the celebrated 'C vs S' case. In February 1987 Oxford student Robert Carver used the law and the media to try to force his former girlfriend into abandoning her planned abortion. Carver lost his legal struggle to prove that abortion after 18 weeks was not permissible under the 1929 Infant Life (Preservation) Act, when three court of appeal judges ruled that the 18-21 week old fetus was incapable of being born alive. But he won the battle to terrify the woman out of her rights. She was too traumatised by the press witch-hunt, orchestrated by the anti-abortion lobby, to go ahead with the abortion. The baby is now living with the self-righteous Carver, while the reluctant mother has dropped out of college and gone into hiding to recover from her ordeal. Carver's legal moves cost an estimated £50 000, but it is generally assumed that the Society for the Protection of the Unborn Child picked up the tab. The smug postgraduate is now being held up as a shining example of caring fatherhood, and his daughter as an example of why abortion should not happen, by David Alton in *his* battle to win the holy war against abortion.

Cases such as these have been exploited to full effect by the anti-abortion groups. Spuc, the first anti-abortion group, was launched in

Pro-life propaganda: upholding the rights of the fetus means denying the rights of women

a blaze of publicity at a press conference in the house of commons in January 1967. Its initial aim was to prevent the passage of Liberal MP David Steel's abortion bill. Once the bill became law later that year, Spuc made reform of the 1967 Act its immediate aim and its repeal a long-term ideal. Spuc's principal founders were Phyllis Bowman and Elspeth Rhys Williams, under whose leadership it has developed into a highly effective pressure group. Today the organisation has an income of £750 000 a year, 40 000 members and a staff of 21.

Life is the second major anti-abortion group, founded in 1970. Like Spuc its immediate aim is to oppose the 1967 Act, although it is more fundamentalist in its attitude to abortion. The group was formed by breakaway Spuc members who felt their old organisation was too cautious and negative. Its first national chairman John Scarisbrick was of the belief that it was not enough to campaign against abortion—Life set out to help women with unwanted pregnancies by providing advice and sometimes short-term housing. Like Spuc, Life is now a formidable lobby group and an expert in promoting its cause. It has an annual income of £126 000 (and that of its charitable wing £108 000) and a membership of 30 000.

The issue is women's rights

The moralists have succeeded in creating a false debate around the issue of abortion. They have elevated the question of the rights of the fetus and removed the question of women's rights from the agenda of public debate. Alton's insistence on the rights of the fetus means denying the right of women to play a full role in society. In responding to the debate on abortion our aim should be to steer the discussion away from the spheres of theology and medicine and into the political arena. We need to show that the consequence of the controversy over abortion, and any legislation that flows from it, can only be to reinforce the oppression of women in British society.

David Alton insists on the absolute right to life from the moment of conception onwards, and regards the fetus as a potential human being which has the same right to life as any person. It is true that a fetus is a potential adult person. But whether or not that potential is realised depends on a wide range of social factors.

If, for example, the fetus has been conceived by a woman who is poor or working class in the third world or the West, then its chances of achieving adulthood are much lower than if it is in the womb of a woman of higher social position. For the majority of women in the world, their pregnancies are as likely to end in miscarriages, still-births, neo-natal or infant deaths, as they are to result in a healthy adult. In Britain a fetus is significantly more likely to become an adult if it is conceived by a woman from the propertied, business or professional classes than if it is conceived by a working class woman. A baby born prematurely—or with a congenital heart defect—is more likely to survive if its parents live near a teaching hospital with a specialist unit, or if they are members of Bupa. If a baby is born with severe abnormalities it is likely to be judged to be incapable of realising its full human potential. In line with long-established medical practice, it will be allowed to die. Nor is the right to life absolute even when adulthood has been achieved.

In the deeply Christian American South, black people who are convicted of killing white people are likely to find themselves deprived of their right to life in the electric chair. In Belfast or Derry teenage joy-riders are likely to be shot on sight with plastic bullets by the enforcers of the same moral code that is so zealously upheld by the pro-life lobby. In the West Bank and the Gaza Strip and throughout the Middle East, human life is considered expendable in the cause of upholding Western interests by military might.

The notion of the sanctity of the life of a human individual, at any stage of its development from embryo to geriatric, is a metaphysical concept. In the real world, the potential of human life is only realised in society, in the interaction of the individual with other human beings. Nowhere is the *social* character of human life more apparent than in the way that the relationship of a potential mother to a fetus determines its status in society. The crucial distinction here is between a woman whose pregnancy is wanted and one who conceives an unwanted pregnancy.

A woman who sets out to become pregnant welcomes every day after the first missed period and greets a positive pregnancy test with delight. She is eager to relay the good news to her partner, to her family and friends. She will make enthusiastic preparations for the birth, even begin choosing names. For her and for all around her, this fetus is already perceived as a baby and everybody begins the process of developing a relationship to it as a human person. The pleased-to-be-pregnant woman flaunts her growing abdomen in maternity clothes and is showered with presents, goodwill and social approval. Contrast the happily pregnant woman with the woman who conceives by accident or mishap. Every day that the period is late causes growing fear and apprehension and the positive test provokes only horror. She may be unable to tell anybody of her plight, perhaps least of all the putative father or her own family. Thinking of a name for the potential child will be the last thing on her mind. Feeling sick, frightened and alone, she may be forced to conceal all these and her increasing girth from the world of employers, husbands, fathers, even friends. Whereas the woman with a wanted pregnancy goes through a life-enhancing experience, the woman with an unwanted pregnancy experiences her pregnancy as life-threatening.

Those who proclaim the abstract moral absolute of the right to life uphold the potential life of the fetus in the womb against the actual life of the woman in society. The former is a potential human existence, the latter a real human being whose potential for development in society is in danger of being constrained by the burden of child-bearing and child-rearing that our society imposes on women. For us the key issue is not when human life begins. For us the only issue is the question of women's rights and how to defend them.

Reverse into the future

The anti-abortionists have yet to meet their ambition of destroying the Abortion Act. But they have certainly forced their opponents on to the defensive. The campaign against the Alton Bill reveals a remarkable retreat by the left and the women's movement from the sort of movement in defence of abortion rights around which they could mobilise tens of thousands of people a decade ago.

In 1975 the National Abortion Campaign was founded with the central slogan 'Free Abortion on Demand, A Woman's Right to Choose'. The immediate issue which led to the formation of NAC was James White's attempt to tighten up the 1967 Abortion Act. NAC insisted that its opposition to White could not be restricted to a defence of the 1967 Act. It called for women's access to abortion on demand and particularly upset its more moderate supporters by appealing for abortion up to full term (see David Marsh & Joanna Chambers, *Abortion Politics,* 1981).

By 1979 and the introduction of the Corrie Bill under a new Tory government, NAC had shifted ground. Its campaign against Corrie called for 'A Woman's Right to Choose', and dropped the slogan for 'Free Abortion on Demand'. The campaign's focus on cultivating influential allies succeeded in attracting TUC and Labour Party support and in out-lobbying the anti-abortion campaigners. Many NAC supporters thought that trading principles in return for a labour movement mobilisation against Corrie was a price worth

By making abortion an issue of
individual *choice,* the women's
movement has shifted the focus away
from the question of women's *rights*

paying. The opposition of key sections of the medical profession and some skilful parliamentary manoeuvring by Labour left MPs Jo Richardson and Ian Mikardo ensured Corrie's defeat. Others in the women's movement began to feel uncomfortable with the old slogans. Eileen Fairweather felt there was a tendency 'to pose abortion as though it were an end in itself': ' "Free Abortion on Demand", the second demand of the women's liberation movement, has something of that ring; the trouble with all slogans, of course, is that they are shorthand for something more complex, but I know my "Abortion—A Woman's Right to Choose" badge always produced more sympathetic chats on the bus' ('Abortion: The Feelings behind the Slogans', *Spare Rib,* October 1979).

While Corrie might have been defeated in parliament, his arguments were never defeated politically. Indeed by shifting the focus of the campaign away from the working class question of *women's rights* to the middle class preoccupation with *individual choice,* the women's movement and the left had conceded vital ground to the right. The way was open for feminist anti-abortionists to argue that the fetus also had the right to choose. Other sections of the movement could also interpret the issue according to their own individualistic concerns. Black women noted that in some instances they were encouraged to have abortions in the same way that they were pressed into contraception and sterilisation—as part of a racist establishment drive to curb the black population. Some black women's groups concluded that rather than defending women's right to abortion they should take a more sympathetic view of moves to restrict it. Disabled women interpreted developments in the diagnosis of fetal abnormalities, allowing for termination even quite late in pregnancy, as a denial of their status. Insisting on the rights of babies to be born with congenital defects, they also opposed demands for abortion rights. These subjective responses to the abortion issue reinforced the divisive thrust of establishment anti-abortion propaganda and helped to fragment the resistance of the women's movement.

The question of abortion as a *necessity* for working class women was ignored and the importance of fighting for the *right* to abortion on demand was lost. The dangerous consequences of this approach have been fully borne out in the campaign against the Alton Bill.

Nine years of Thatcher's rule have shifted the climate of opinion even more in favour of the anti-abortion lobby. Opinion polls appear to confirm a greater degree of popular support for some restriction on abortion laws, though the right has by no means won the argument. Unlike in the seventies, the TUC and the Labour leadership are much too frightened of standing outside the new moral consensus to take a stand on a controversial issue like abortion. Indeed, the TUC seems to be moribund and its leader Norman Willis a figure of fun. Apart from a few individuals like Jo Richardson and Clare Short, the Labour Party has avoided the abortion issue. Even the medical profession, already bruised in a number of encounters with the government, seems inclined to accept some compromise over Alton's Bill in a way it was not over earlier attempts to interfere with its powers over abortion.

In contrast to the seventies the opportunism of the left and the women's movement is unlikely even to produce results today. There is now little scope for compromise over the abortion issue. The moralists are in the ascendant and are dictating harsh terms. Yet the left and the women's movement are still playing by the rules established in the late seventies. From the outset the official campaign against the Alton Bill emphasised the importance of being reasonable so as not to alienate more conservative potential allies who were still prepared to countenance abortion. The leadership of the opposition to Alton was intent on appealing to an illusory middle ground and a liberal sentiment that no longer exists. It cautioned against a forceful assertion of women's right to abortion on demand, and urged its supporters to close ranks around a defence of the 1967 Act. 'Why are we working so hard to defend such a flawed act against this latest attack?' asked Leonora Lloyd of the Fight the Alton Bill campaign (*Socialist Outlook,* November/December 1987). No satisfactory answer was forthcoming. We can only conclude that the left and the women's movement believe that it is no longer possible to do anything positive to take the fight for abortion rights forward.

The modest ambitions of the anti-Alton mainstream were evident in its conciliatory response to the questions of late abortion and fetal rights. Almost every article commissioned by the press from Alton's opponents was prefaced with the phrase 'We do not like late abortions...'. Almost every argument made concessions to the idea that the time-limit should be reduced to 24 weeks, so long as it was made easier to arrange abortions earlier. Thus Glynis Donovan of the Women's Reproductive Rights Information Centre explained that some doctors were 'exerting pressure on the issue of the viability of the fetus'. Her view? 'We are not unsympathetic to that: our point is that if the system works properly, very few women should be having late abortions' (*New Statesman,* 15 January 1988). Certainly we want to see improvements in the system to allow for early abortions, but not at the expense of women's right to have an abortion whenever they need it.

Another indication of the retreat from the ideals of the past was the way in which the opposition to Alton presented its timid defence of abortion rights in terms of conscience or individual rights. Labour MP Tony Blair provided the most cringing demonstration of the first offence. 'Personally I have found it an agonising decision' he pleaded in an article that was supposed to put the case against Alton. 'We recognise that we are resolving a conflict,' he continued, 'between the rights of the woman and those of the fetus or unborn child.' Blair's dilemma was how to decide 'when the one prevails over the other'. If a woman who knows that she is carrying a baby that will be born severely handicapped has an abortion, concluded Blair, 'I do not say she is right,' but 'I cannot in conscience, as a legislator, say that I can take that decision for her' (*The Times,* 19 January 1988). This feeble and equivocal defence of abortion contrasts dramatically with the confident assertiveness of the anti-abortion lobby. Labour MP Clare Short also reduced the whole issue to individual agonies of conscience, arguing that 'each woman has to reach her own decision within the framework of the present law: that is how it should remain' (*Guardian,* 10 October 1987). The appreciation that abortion is a working class question of women's rights has entirely disappeared from the arguments of the opposition.

The official campaign against Alton also concealed the central issue of women's rights through a narrow focus on the exceptional victims of the Alton Bill. In a move calculated to appeal to sympathy and moralism, the left and the women's movement highlighted the plight of the most vulnerable women—the disadvantaged who cannot cope with pregnancy, those facing the distress of giving birth to a severely handicapped baby, teenagers or menopausal women who often fail to acknowledge or recognise pregnancy. The feminist gynaecologist Wendy Savage, leading campaigner in Doctors for Choice, declared that 'it is always the most deprived women, usually with housing problems or of low intelligence, who are involved' (*The Times,* 29 September 1987). Clare Short continually pointed to the problems confronting women who discover they are carrying an abnormal fetus. Harriet Harman sprang to the defence of young women who do not face up to the fact that they are pregnant and older women who mistake pregnancy for the menopause. While these are all genuine problems, the focus on them neglects the much greater number of women seeking abortions for none of these reasons, and does not strengthen our case against Alton.

The most serious deficiency of the campaign against Alton has been its downgrading of the issue of women's rights. For us, abortion is not just a question of protecting the most vulnerable women from the trauma of an unwanted pregnancy. Abortion is a question of the rights of women and our ability to organise against our oppression. Unless we make this the focus of debate we will never build a movement for women's rights nor defeat our opponents.

Is the 1967 Act worth defending?

Faced with an attack on abortion rights the natural inclination of many women is simply to defend the existing provisions. But we need to go much further if we are to defeat the anti-abortion lobby. Fighting for free abortion on demand is the only position consistent with a defence of women's rights. In fighting for free abortion on demand we should be clear that a celebration of the virtues of the 1967 Act will get us nowhere. This is because the 1967 Abortion Act negates the very concept of abortion on demand. How can we fight for abortion on demand by defending a law that never granted it in the first place? If we fudge the issue we will hand the initiative to our opponents and we will lose. We only need to look at why the 1967 Act was passed in the first place to see the deficiencies of the legislation from the point of view of women fighting for emancipation.

The main pressure for the 1967 Act was the establishment's concern to curb the fertility of women whom the state considered feckless or irresponsible in the use of contraceptives. In the fifties and sixties a growing range of social problems—'unmarried mothers', 'juvenile delinquents', 'latchkey kids', 'problem families'—became a focus of professional concern. Large families came to be associated with poverty, and poverty with crime. Part of the solution to what came to be known as the 'cycle of deprivation'—the reproduction of social problems within working class families—was stricter control over reproduction. In a long debate in the house of lords in October 1967, Lady Somerskill (Labour) said that she was concerned with the 'masses of people who lived in the industrial areas of the towns':

'The slums, where adolescents slept in the same room and where families were kept awake at night by a crying child. We plead for those families where the family is already so big that the wife is harassed and where the husband is so bad-tempered that he stays out at night in the public house, arrives home drunk, has sexual intercourse, and produces another child.' (Cited in the *British Medical Journal,* 28 October 1967)

The state was concerned to eliminate as far as possible 'undesirable' and 'undesired' pregnancies. In the same year as the 1967 Abortion Act was passed, the National Health Service (Family Planning) Act became law. This allowed district health authorities to provide family planning advice on the NHS, and contraceptives to be supplied to married women. This was later extended to unmarried women. Abortion came to be regarded as necessary for those who neglected to make use of these facilities.

Lord Soper said he was not concerned with 'promiscuous girls of 15 or 16 or frivolous married women who were pregnant by a man other than their husband, but with the 80 per cent of abortion cases involving women for whom another pregnancy was an intolerable prospect' (cited in the *British Medical Journal*, 28 October 1967). Labour MP Dr John Dunwoody said that he supported the bill on social, not medical, grounds for similar reasons. He expressed a hope that it would lead to a reconstitution of proper family life:

'In many over-large families the mother was so broken physically and emotionally with the continual bearing of children that it became impossible for her to fulfil her real and worthwhile function of holding together the family unit, and for this reason there were so many problem families.' (Cited in the *British Medical Journal*, 30 July 1966)

This too was the concern of home secretary Roy Jenkins who put up a staunch defence of the social clause on the grounds that 'many women far from anxious to escape the responsibilities of motherhood, but wishing to discharge existing ones more effectively, would be denied relief' without it (cited in the *British Medical Journal*, 30 July 1966). The state sanctioned the Abortion Act as a device to regulate the dissolute habits of the working class and to improve the standards of family life.

A new law was also necessary to regulate the availability of abortions. Existing legislation was inadequate to prevent the large number of backstreet abortions or to stamp out illegal operations by members of the medical profession. Home secretary Jenkins described the law as 'uncertain, harsh, archaic and in urgent need of reform' (*British Medical Journal*, 30 July 1966). In 1949 one study by Dr Eustace Chesser estimated that 250 000 abortions were taking place every year. The practice of disguising medical abortions as 'D & Cs' (scrapes) became commonplace. The do-it-yourself abortion—using syringes or knitting needles which often left women infected, perforated or bleeding badly—was widespread. Although there were many abortions, prosecutions were rare. Probably one in every thousand came to light because the woman died. The Act aimed to bring abortion firmly under the control of the state. The *British Medical Journal* declared that 'the medical profession subscribes fully to the admirable aim of putting the backstreet abortionist out of business.' The Act and its administration made sure that abortion became the business of the medical profession instead.

The 1967 Act also aimed to address the problem of children born with physical and mental disabilities. A series of Rubella outbreaks in the early sixties (leading to babies being born deaf and blind) and the terrible effects of the Thalidomide drug which became apparent at the same time, as well as the prevalence of Downs Syndrome and spina bifida, prompted intensive research into the early detection of congenital and genetic abnormalities. Doctors wanted the right to terminate pregnancy when there was a high risk of abnormality. Before 1967, abortion on these grounds was illegal, and a woman had to convince three doctors, one of them a psychiatrist, that the *thought* of having an abnormal child was gravely affecting *her* mental health.

The issue of women's rights never even entered into the discussions leading up to the passage of the 1967 Act, except in a proscriptive sense. Many members of the medical profession objected to the social clause on the grounds that it would open the way to 'abortion on demand' (see correspondence in the *British Medical Journal,* 31 December 1966). The newly formed Society for the Protection of the Unborn Child presented its statement on the bill which was given prominent space in the *Lancet,* warning that the bill would lead to unnecessary deaths and 'abortion on demand' (14 January 1967). There were prolonged debates in parliament and outside it on how to translate social considerations into law without granting easy access to abortion. After three mornings of controversy and seven votes during the committee stage of the bill in February, the final form of words was agreed. David Steel, the architect of the bill, was at pains to reassure his critics that there was no possibility of 'abortion on demand': 'It is not the intention of the promoters of the abortion bill to leave a wider door open for abortion on request' (cited in Victoria Greenwood & Jock Young, *Abortion on Demand,* 1976). While Steel opposes the Alton Bill, in the recent debates he has repeatedly restated his opposition to women having the right to abortion.

Time to fight for real freedom

Anybody committed to the cause of women's liberation will agree that the 1967 Act cannot meet our needs. It does not give women abortion on demand: the law was finely tuned to make sure that this possibility would never arise. It does not give us control: the purpose of the new law was to hand control to the state and the medical profession. It does not give us the facilities we need: abortion services are the first casualties of the cuts, and more women are being forced to pay for a service that should be freely available.

Defending an Act that denies women the chance to control their fertility is simply a strategy for perpetuating our problems. Worse still, it hands the initiative to our opponents to launch a further legal assault. We need to fight for free abortion on demand to free women from the bind of child-bearing and child-rearing, and to escape from the drudgery of domestic work. We need free abortion on demand to free women from economic dependence on men, and to improve our chances of finding decent employment. We need free abortion on demand most of all to free women to play a wider role in political life, and to enable us to start organising resistance to oppression.

Fighting for all these things means making a stand against the moralists. Today there is no possibility of achieving real freedom unless we are prepared to fight and fight hard. The champions of the new morality no longer bother to hide what they are about. There is no more 'live and let live'. It has become acceptable to label abortion as 'sinful'. It has become acceptable to preach intolerance against 'sinners'. The moralists demand an equally forceful response and we should make no attempt to hide our objectives. We know that there is no going back to the 'good old days' of liberalism. They were never all that good anyway for women. For us free abortion on demand is not negotiable.

**Fighting for free abortion on demand
is the only way to beat the moralists**

5.
Going on the offensive

The arguments of the new moralists have gained a hearing, not because they have any inherent merit and least of all because they make sense, but because they have yet to be answered. As the establishment steps up its crusade to outlaw 'permissiveness', we have to make our voices heard if we are to beat back reaction and advance the cause of human emancipation. The platform below outlines the strategy we need to adopt to counter the moral offensive. We need to:

● **Expose the official view of family life**
We are not against the family as such: for many people the family is a refuge from the stresses and strains of life under capitalism. But we are opposed to the family as an instrument for perpetuating the exploitation of the working class, and as a device for suppressing the class struggle and restricting the rights of women, lesbians and gay men. Fighting for an end to exploitation and oppression means exposing the reality of family life every time the ruling class seeks to force its views upon us.

● Defend democratic rights

The capitalist system claims to champion the ideals of equality and freedom, but in practice denies these basic rights to certain sections of society. Our view is that democratic rights are neither divisible nor negotiable. A movement which seeks to unite the working class against the system must make it a priority to uphold the rights of the oppressed to equal treatment in society and to campaign for the rights of women, lesbians, gay men and other oppressed groups.

● Fight for free contraception and abortion on demand

The mounting offensive against women's access to contraception and abortion should make us all the more determined to launch a counter-offensive around these issues. Anybody old enough to have sex is old enough to have access to the facilities to cope with the consequences. Every woman should be able to demand abortion without seeking permission from a doctor and without legislative restriction. Pregnancy testing should be free: currently used tests involve delays and expense—the most efficient tests should be made available for the earliest possible detection of pregnancy. The fact that contraceptive failure is the most common reason for abortion is a strong argument for integrating the services, which should be separate from maternity wards, and which should provide access to all women who need to prevent or terminate pregnancy.

● Campaign for the decriminalisation of homosexuality

The Tories have made it clear that they aim to outlaw homosexuality. The current law embodied in the 1967 Sexual Offences Act merely exempted homosexual behaviour in certain strictly defined situations. Through Clause 28 of the Local Government Bill, the Tories are seeking to impose even more stringent conditions on the public presentation of homosexuality. The only effective rejoinder is a campaign demanding full equality for lesbians and gays. We should be fighting for the removal of Clause 28 and the complete decriminalisation of homosexuality.

● Oppose all forms of state interference

Today the authorities are promoting a series of moral panics to justify the extension of the state's repressive apparatus into all aspects of working class life. Our starting point must be one of unequivocal opposition to all forms of state interference. We should take a stand against attempts to introduce widespread censorship of books, television and films in the wake of panics about sex and violence. We should resist all attempts to use the child abuse hysteria as a vehicle for extending the powers of social workers, police and the courts to step up surveillance of family life. Inviting the state to step up its policing powers can only undermine our ability to organise resistance to state attacks on a whole number of issues, from the poll tax to NHS cuts.

● **Organise in the working class**
The working class is the only force in society which stands to gain from overturning the official morality, and the only agency capable of mounting an effective resistance to state attacks. We have to convince activists in our local communities and in the labour movement that the debate about morality is something of decisive importance for the working class. We have to spread the struggle against oppression among a much wider audience if we are to build a united resistance movement against attacks on women, lesbians and gay men. Once the working class is won over to the cause of women's liberation and homosexual emancipation, there will be nothing the moralists can do to save their rotten old conventions or their decaying system.

Appendix

After the 1967 Act, the legal offensive

A rearguard action by an assortment of reactionaries to restrict abortion rights began almost as soon as the 1967 Abortion Act became law. Liberal MP David Steel's Medical Termination of Pregnancy Bill received the royal assent on 27 October 1967 and came into force as the 1967 Abortion Act from April 1968. The anti-abortionists had put up a stiff opposition to the bill as it passed through its various stages to the statute book, and they were not prepared to give up without a fight. Although they made no headway in their efforts to change the law, the succession of anti-abortion bills that came before parliament served as a focus for the energetic activities of the pro-life lobby.

1969: Tory MP Norman St John Stevas introduced his 10-minute rule bill stipulating that one of the two doctors required to sign the abortion order should be an NHS consultant, or a doctor of equivalent status. This amendment had been promoted by the medical associations and debated at length, before being defeated at the committee stage of the Steel Bill. It failed to get through its first reading by 11 votes.

1970: Tory MP Bryant Godman Irvine introduced a similar measure the following year. Its sponsors were aware that it had no chance of progressing anywhere. But their aim was simply to air the abortion issue in parliament once again and test out opinion. As future years would show, the pro-life lobby would lose no opportunity for raising their profile. The bill was talked out.

1971: The Medical Services (Referral) Bill, to prohibit the charging of fees for referring or recommending persons to doctors or clinics for treatment, was presented by Tory MP John Hunt. Hunt's bill excluded charities from this prohibition. It was given a formal first reading, but was never debated, and failed to reach its second reading.

1973: A second bill brought forward by Tory member Michael Grylls duplicated Hunt's except that it did include charities. The Abortion (Amendment) Bill fell with the dissolution of parliament in February 1974. It was reintroduced in May 1974 and was given an unopposed second reading. Meanwhile, under pressure from the anti-abortion lobby, the government appointed the Lane committee to examine the operation of the 1967 Act. It sat for two and a half years and was unanimous in approving the operation of the Act. It recommended an amendment to the 1929 Infant Life (Preservation) Act to reduce the time-limit for legal abortions from 28 to 24 weeks. But this did not satisfy the pro-life lobby. Its answer to the Lane committee was *Babies for Burning,* a scurrilous book alleging that aborted fetuses were being made into soap, left screaming on draining boards and thrown into buckets, etc.

1974: Labour MP for Glasgow Pollok James White introduced a private member's bill which aimed to cut the number of abortions by half. The bill sought to remove the so-called social clause of the 1967 Act and replace it with the specification that abortion was only legal if there was a 'grave' risk to life or a 'serious' risk to health. It aimed to prevent referral bureaus being financially associated with abortion clinics and laid down statutory conditions for the approval of private clinics. The White Bill was given a second reading by a majority of 203 to 88, and shocked supporters of the 1967 Act. The National Abortion Campaign was formed to resist the bill. In February 1975 White withdrew his bill after the Labour government agreed to appoint a select committee to examine his proposals. In November 1976 the committee recommended that there should be legislation to reduce the time-limit to 20 weeks, that it should be easier for doctors and nurses to claim conscientious objection to carrying out abortions and that abortion clinics, referral agencies and pregnancy testing centres should be licensed.

1977: Tory MP and Spuc activist William Benyon introduced a private member's bill based on the first report of the select committee. It would have had less effect on the operation of the 1967 Act than White's bill, but it would have restricted the availability of abortions substantially. The Benyon Bill was given a second reading by 170 votes to 132. It was the first amendment bill to reach and complete its committee stage. The bill came out of committee largely unscathed, but there was no available time for its report stage. The government refused to give it time, so it fell at the end of parliament. But it was a useful experience for the anti-abortion lobby in learning the art of committee-room manoeuvring.

1978: Sir Bernard Braine introduced a 10-minute bill, the provisions of which followed closely those of the Benyon Bill. As a 10-minute bill it had no chance of progressing, but Braine was given leave to introduce it, with 181 voting in favour and 175 against.

1979: Tory John Corrie introduced a bill to radically amend the 1967 Act and the 1929 Infant Life (Preservation) Act. It introduced a time-limit of 20 weeks into the legislation, with the sole exception that an abortion could be carried out legally up to 28 weeks if two doctors decided in good faith that the child would be born severely handicapped. It aimed to eliminate the social clause, and replace it with two sub-clauses which would make abortion legal in far fewer circumstances. It amended the 'conscience clause' so that any doctor or nurse could refuse to take part in abortion operations on moral grounds. It aimed to tighten up the licensing procedure for clinics and advice or referral bureaus, and, more importantly, to separate referral agencies from clinics carrying out abortions. The bill got through its second reading by a majority of 242 votes to 98, the largest majority any amendment bill had enjoyed at its second reading. The bill was substantially amended in committee, and fell when it failed to complete its report stage. After the prolonged saga of the Corrie Bill many uncommitted MPs grew weary of the abortion issue. The pro-life lobby had to wait five years for their next big chance to make abortion an issue.

1985: Enoch Powell's Unborn Children (Protection) Bill called for a ban on 'pure' embryo research and proposed that all doctors carrying out *in-vitro* fertilisation must get the written permission of the secretary of state before implanting a named woman with an embryo. Powell's bill aimed to give rights to embryos from conception, with the implication that post-coital contraception and abortion could be deemed illegal. Although it won a huge majority on its second reading in February 1985, there was never much chance of it becoming law. Its role was to stir up prejudice about evil scientists cloning embryos or creating hybrids or otherwise tampering with the species. Powell's appeal to backward fears about science and technology had the desired effect. Two million people signed a petition to parliament backing his bill. The issue of embryo experimentation is on the parliamentary agenda once again. The Tories produced a white paper in November 1987 which largely follows the recommendations of the Warnock committee which was set up in 1982 to inquire into new reproductive techniques, surrogacy and embryo research. The government intends to produce the Warnock and Powell alternatives on embryology separately from the issues of surrogacy and IVF, and let MPs choose between them as a matter of individual conscience.

1986: The Bishop of Birmingham, Hugh Montefiore, introduced his Infant Life (Preservation) Bill to amend the 1929 Act by outlawing terminations after 24 weeks in the house of lords. It passed its second reading in January 1987 and would normally have gone on to the committee stage on the floor of the house. Lord Houghton of Sowerby, the veteran pro-life campaigner, pointed out to William Whitelaw, the former deputy prime minister and leader of the lords, that there were problems. The opponents of the bill had it in their power to prolong discussion enough to wreck the timetable for the government's main legislative programme, and with it Mrs Thatcher's option for a June general election. He suggested the alternative of a small select committee which could examine the issue and make proposals. The committee's deliberations were ended by the dissolution of parliament for the general election.

1987: Tory Nicholas Winterton prepared to introduce a private member's bill to prevent doctors referring women for abortions if they are linked commercially to the people who carry them out. This is designed to upset the standard referral procedures operated by the British Pregnancy

Advisory Service and other abortion charities. It follows the recommendations of the 1976 report of the select committee on abortion.

1987: Lord Houghton of Sowerby has taken up word for word the legislation sponsored in the last parliament by the Bishop of Birmingham. When parliament resumed after the election Houghton arranged for the select committee to reconvene to pursue its work. Since Montefiore had retired, however, and no other bishop was willing to do the job, Houghton retabled the bill himself.

1987: In October Liberal MP David Alton introduced his private member's bill to outlaw abortion after 18 weeks' gestation. In January 1988 it passed its second reading with a majority of 45, larger than expected. It is likely to be amended in the committee stage to set the limit at 24 weeks.

1987: Two other MPs preparing bills dealing with the abortion issue were successful in the private members' ballot. Tory backbencher Edward Leigh's bill would require clinics to be licensed to perform abortions on women from overseas. They would have to arrange aftercare for their patients by referring them to a medical practitioner in their own country. Failure to do so would mean loss of licence. The other anti-abortion MP planning legislation is Tory Ken Hind.

Weekly paper of the
Revolutionary Communist Party

the next step is the paper that covers all aspects of the establishment's moral offensive, from the Aids scare to the abortion issue, and presents the working class view of sex and family life. Don't be without it.

- 40p weekly
- Subscriptions cost £26 for a year to anywhere in Britain and Ireland

Write to Junius Publications, BCM JPLtd, London WC1N 3XX. Phone (01) 729 3771.